Wild Days

Wild Days

Outdoor play for young adventurers

Richard Irvine

Contents

Introduction

Wild Days is for anyone who wants to get outside, explore and have an adventure. Crammed full of fun ideas to do outdoors and craft projects using natural found materials, it's the perfect companion if you want a break from the world of phones, consoles and TV. From cooking toffee apples on a fire to painting with earth; from racing twig boats down river to carving walking sticks; and making your own rope swing or taking time to chill under a tree, there's something here for everyone to have a go at.

Every day can be a wild day. The wilderness is not always on our doorstep, but little bits of wild nature can be found everywhere – whether you live in a bustling city or its suburbs, or close to farms, forests or the coast. There are adventures to be had in parks, on city streets, canal tow-paths, riverbanks, beaches, woods, moorland and country walks. All that is needed is a bit of curiosity and maybe a guide like this book.

Many of the projects in this book can be completed for free or with very few resources. However, a few simple tools and supplies can make your time outside even more enjoyable. This book outlines what equipment you could use and how best to use it, with detailed step-by-step guides and clear photographs. But encouraging creativity is at the heart of every project, so feel free to improvise and use what you can find. The process of discovery is more important than making a beautiful finished thing. Whatever happens, there is something to be learned from every adventure. It doesn't always matter where you go or what you do; the most important thing is to get out and do something.

Having worked and played outside all my life, I know that being out in the fresh air, surrounded by nature, is good for our bodies and our minds. Learning about our neighbourhood nature connects us to where we live and makes us feel more at home. The more time you spend outdoors, the more you notice the patterns of the changing seasons; get to know the sights, sounds and smells of your local wildlife; and enjoy 'slow time' as you lose yourself in the fascination of nature.

As you start to do some of the activities in this book, look around and try to name some of the plants and animals that you go past or see in the sky above you. You might be pleasantly surprised to realise you already know more about your local wildlife than you think. There is, however, no need to get hung up on the naming of things. Sometimes, learning the name of plants and animals is interesting for its own sake. It can also help us to communicate about the things that matter to us. But the pressure to name everything you see can be a barrier to finding out more. Focus on getting to know the names of things that you need to know and want to find out about. I like making things from wood, so I need to know which tree is which, and what features make it good for a particular job.

If the outdoors seems like a frightening place, go for a walk somewhere you know really well first, then start exploring new places with friends or family. Always let an adult know where you are going and when you will be back. Ask for help with a project if you are finding it difficult and get into the habit of asking yourself 'What if...' questions. For example, 'What if my knife slips?', 'What if the fire's still hot?' so that you think ahead to avoid things going wrong and stay safe.

A note to the adults...

To be safe in the world, young people need to be allowed to take risks. If they grow up insulated from potential harm, they may find it difficult to assess what is safe or dangerous for themselves and not learn to ask the important 'What if...' questions that help us to consider the consequences of our actions and to make good decisions. Some of the projects and ideas in this book involve hazards, such as fire, tools and getting lost, but all can be undertaken without harm if safety advice is followed and common sense used. You know your young people and the context. My plea is to let them explore and experiment with the ideas in this book. Join in alongside or keep an eye from a distance, but try to relax, enjoy being outdoors with them and remember that the benefits of outdoor play and adventure will stand them in good stead for the bigger challenges ahead.

Behaving responsibly outdoors

This book is full of interesting things for you to do and learn about outdoors. On your wild days out, it is very important to remember that the world is not a playground for humans but the habitat for us and all other living things. At the very least, we should try to leave little or no trace of our activities. It would be fantastic if we could leave things in an even better state than we found them and to have a positive impact on our environment.

The way that you will do this will depend on what you are doing and where you are. We will need to behave differently on some abandoned ground near a construction site than we would in a fragile wilderness ecosystem.

You can find out more from outdoor recreation and wildlife organizations in your area about how to do the right thing in your local area, but these general rules are worth following:

- Collecting materials – take only small amounts of things that are very plentiful, use fallen wood or prune trees at the right time of year.
- Lighting fires – leave no trace (see page 36).
- Tidying up – if you brought it with you, take it home with you.
- Going to the toilet – wee far away from streams and rivers. Dig a hole and bury your poo and toilet roll.
- Getting to and from places – if you can walk, cycle, scoot or skate there then do. If not, try to use public transport.
- Buying clothing and equipment for your adventures – use what you have, borrow from friends or buy secondhand if you can.

Many countries have a countryside code. In the UK it asks us to respect other people, protect the natural environment and to enjoy the outdoors.

Leave no trace

The Leave No Trace Center for Outdoor Ethics in the USA has developed these seven principles:
1. Plan ahead and prepare.
2. Travel and camp on durable surfaces.
3. Dispose of waste properly.
4. Leave what you find.
5. Minimize campfire impacts.
6. Respect wildlife.
7. Be considerate of other visitors.

'Leave No Trace is a framework for making good decisions about enjoying the outdoors responsibly. All who enjoy spending time in the outdoors, regardless of how we choose to do so, are sharing a finite amount of land. We have to both do what we can to minimize our cumulative impacts over time while also striving to wisely use/enjoy the natural resources. Our collective goal is to be good stewards of the natural world around us.'
For more information, visit: www.LNT.org

Adventurer's kit bag

What you will need for an adventure will depend on where you are going, how long for, what you want to do, and what the weather will be like. Be prepared for things to change, especially the weather, and have more than you might need. Saying that, there is no need to take the kitchen sink.

These are a few of the things you might think about taking with you on a tiny adventure, but there should be no need to feel like you have to buy fancy, expensive equipment to explore and play outdoors. You don't want to be one of those people with all the gear and no idea!

The basics

- Clothing and footwear for any conditions you might expect to find. It is no fun being wet, cold or sunburnt. In some places it can feel like you experience four seasons in one day.
- If you will be out in the sun, cover up, wear a hat and use high-factor sunscreen.
- In the woods, I always wear long trousers. They protect from stinging, scratching plants and biting insects. Biting insects about? Get some insect repellent.
- A small rucksack to carry any spare clothes, tools, supplies, snacks, water bottle, etc.
- Water bottle or a flask of hot drink.
- Fire-lighting kit, including a striker, tinder and newspaper. This is something that you can keep changing as you develop your fire-lighting skills.

- If you are using any tools (see page 16) then it is really important to carry (and know how to use) a small first aid kit with at least some plasters, non-adhesive dressings, micropore tape, a couple of sterile dressings, cleansing wipes, tweezers and scissors. Hopefully you never need to open it – just make sure it is with you in case you ever do. Know the local emergency phone numbers and how to ask for help.
- A notebook to write down any interesting things that you notice.

Other things you might want to take

- It is always worth having a few supplies that will allow you to be spontaneously creative and top of the list is... string! You can never have enough. I have string in my coat and trouser pockets, rucksacks and in the car and I use it all the time.
- String made from natural fibres like cotton, jute and sisal is great because it will biodegrade over time if it disappears down the river or gets accidentally dropped in the woods.
- Paracord (used on parachutes) is ideal for when stronger cord is needed or as rot-proof cord that can be left out in the rain.
- A strong 65ft- (20m-) long rope that can take a really heavy load is good for making swings (see page 56) and dragging logs around.
- A tarpaulin to sit on, tie up for shelter or to cover your stick den (see page 32) to keep it waterproof.

Safety

Make sure that someone responsible knows where you are going and when you will be back. How will you communicate with them if you need to? Remember that mobile phones can get lost or damaged and the battery won't last forever.

Craft supplies

For many of the projects in this book, you won't need much other than things you find around you and a few basic supplies. Of course, you don't need to take these supplies out with you. You can use them when you return home with the natural materials you have sourced. But if you want to take them, then a sturdy, easy-to-carry bag will be useful.

A few of the projects require specific tools or materials, such as plaster of Paris for casting tracks. These are described on the relevant pages. Other useful items include the following:

- Scissors, card, felt pens and tape
- Calico material or old cotton sheets for leaf bashing (see page 102), flag making (see page 103) and other such things
- Wool of all colours to decorate whatever you make
- Mortar and pestle
- Recycled tubs, jars and containers

Tools

A few simple tools in your bag can expand the opportunities for making and creativity. A small tool bag can travel anywhere with you, just in case you have some spare time and feel like making something.

It is not necessary to spend a fortune when buying new tools but it does makes sense to pay heed to the old adage of 'buy cheap, buy twice'. Sometimes you can hit lucky and find a bargain that will do the job well and last a long time. I always keep my eyes peeled at the recycling centre and at car boot sales and have found many great, if a little neglected, tools over the years. In our throw-away culture, it is very satisfying to find an old tool and restore it back to working order.

Look after the tools you have by keeping them out of contact with stones, soil and moisture. Dry tools after use, apply a little mineral oil to prevent rust and lubricate any moving parts. Store in a safe, dry place that is well out of the reach of small children.

Whittling knife

This is a big topic! To keep things simple, I prefer knives that have a fixed blade over those that fold. To start with, just use whatever knife you have as long as the handle fits your hand and the blade is sharp. If choosing your first knife, consider something like the ones shown top right. From left to right they are a Sloyd, Scout and Companion knife.

There are some links to learn how to keep your knife sharp in the Resources section on page 156. If you want to learn lots more and get into whittling then have a look at *Forest Craft: A Child's Guide to Whittling in the Woodland* (see Resources for more information).

Folding pruning saw

A good pruning saw (see below, right) can be used for cutting small to medium-sized branches. It is easy to carry and the blade folds into the handle, meaning that it can fit into a coat or trouser pocket. All pruning saws should have a way to lock the blade in position when sawing. Some also lock closed to prevent you from opening them by accident. Pruning saws generally cut when pulled rather than pushed; however, some cut on the push and pull cut. It is important to know which you have to avoid bending the blade. A blade with fine teeth will make a cleaner cut, though it will take longer to saw through a larger branch.

Palm drill

This is just a general-purpose drill bit fitted and glued into a handle (see below). They are small, cheap and easy to use but are limited to drilling a single size of hole. They can be purchased from outdoor education equipment suppliers or you can make your own with a file handle, general-purpose or wood drill bit and some 2-part epoxy glue.

Read pages 20–23 to learn how to use these tools safely.

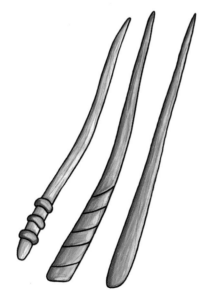

Should I wear gloves when using tools?

It depends how you feel! Wearing safety gloves can help you to feel more confident when using sharp tools but concentrating on what you are doing and using tools safely should protect both your hands without the need for gloves. It is a bad idea to wear a glove on the hand holding a knife or saw, as you will have less grip and therefore control over what you are doing. If you wish to wear a glove on the non-tool hand then it will need to be capable of resisting a cut from the tool you are using. Kevlar gloves will resist slicing and tearing but are little use against points of knives and drill bits which will fit through the weave of the glove material.

Knives and the law

Penalties for breaches of the laws on knives can be serious. Before buying or carrying a knife outside of your own home, it is advisable to be aware of the relevant local laws that apply.

Craft skills

There are lots of different safe ways to use tools and there are also a few, very definitely, unsafe ways. This is a brief introduction to get you started rather than a comprehensive guide.

Staying safe means being mindful of what you are doing and is often a matter of common sense. Common sense, however, is based on experience, so stick with the guidance below until you are practised and confident enough to improvise. If you discover a safe grip or cut that works for you, then feel free to use it. Just always ask yourself the 'What if?' question: 'What if what I'm doing goes wrong?' If it feels dangerous, then it probably is.

Whittling

A few things to remember when using a knife to carve wood that will help keep your first-aid kit zipped shut...

- Sit down when carving.
- Carve away from your body and away from the hand holding the work.
- Use the knife to your side or in front of your knees – NEVER between your legs. EVER! Really, the consequences could be very, very bad.
- Put the knife in its sheath or fold it shut when you are not using it.
- Carve onto something like a stump of wood, a plank or a breadboard.
- Don't put the blade on or in the ground. It will blunt the blade and someone might stand on it. Ouch!

1 Freehand carving

This is just a matter of putting the blade on the wood at the right angle and pushing with the right amount of force. Aim for long, thin shavings rather than trying to carve chunks out of the wood.

2 Knee pull cut

Hold the knife handle in your writing hand with the blade facing away from you. Line your thumb up along the handle and grip the other side with the tips of your fingers. Push the back of the handle into your leg just below your kneecap and keep it there. The knife will stay in this position and not move at all as the wood you are carving is pulled backwards and cut with the underside of the blade. Practise making a point on the end of the stick – first using big, powerful cuts to remove lots of wood, then reducing the force and making smaller and smaller shavings with long, fine, controlled cuts.

3 Stop cut

Place the wood lengthways on a flat stump and press the blade of the knife straight down onto it. Using the part of the blade closest to the handle will allow you to push harder and make a deeper stop cut. Press down with the knife and roll the blade and wood to make a line around as much of the stick as you need to.

This is often followed by using the thumb push to remove wood from one side of the stop cut or for making parallel lines so that you can peel the bark off neatly between them.

4 Thumb push

This technique is a safe and trusty friend but if overused can leave you with a sore thumb. The knife hand just has to hold the blade at the correct angle and barely pushes at all. All the force comes from the thumb of the other hand, which is holding the work. Try to keep the pushing thumb in contact with the handle rather than the metal spine of the knife.

5 Batoning

This is a way of splitting branches lengthways using the knife. Stand the wood you want to split on a flat piece of wood (not the earth, a stone or concrete) and place the blade of the knife across the middle of the piece. Make sure that the blade would pass across the front of your body and not move towards you. Tap the back of the blade with another stick to start a split and keep tapping until the knife blade has moved far enough down the stick to separate the two halves. This technique is not advisable with a folding knife.

6 Drilling

The palm drill is a super-simple tool but it still requires some strength and skill to control. Hold it in the hand you write with, with the work sitting on a flat and stable surface, such as a stump. Drill a hole by pushing downwards while twisting the drill in a clockwise direction. Don't hold the thing you are drilling in your other hand or you might drill a hole in it as well.

7 Sawing

The first thing to think about if you need to saw a piece of wood is how to hold it still. If you have a saw horse then you can saw safely to your heart's content, but it is likely that you will sometimes need to prune a branch from a tree or saw a stick when out for a walk. The key to safety is to hold the wood steady and keep your non-tool hand well out of the way of the saw blade. If the saw jumps out of its cut, it will most likely move towards the middle of your body.

If you need to prune a branch, first find out about your tree and make sure that it is the right time of year to cut wood without harming the tree.

Starting a short distance away from where the branch joins the trunk, saw a third of the way through from the bottom of the branch. Move the saw to the top of the branch, a little bit farther away from the trunk than the undercut and saw downwards until the branch falls.

Tidy up the pruning by sawing the stub of branch off flush with the wrinkly bark collar where the branch left the trunk. This will help it to heal over and protect the tree.

Knots, hitches and lashings

String is your friend but you need to know how to use it and that is where these patterns of twists and turns come in. They can be tricky to learn but once you know them, tying them is like writing your name or riding a bike. All of these examples are used in at least one of the projects. I always think of knots tying cord together, hitches tying a cord to something else, and lashings using cord to join two or more other things together – though usually when we talk about them, we just call them all knots. In the instructions below, the working end of the rope is the one we are moving and using, the standing end of the rope is the other part.

Clove hitch

This hitch has lots of uses, including starting off the square lashing and making tiny rope ladders.

STEP 1

This hitch is tied in the middle of a length of rope to slide over a pole.

STEP 2

Fold the rope to make a loop.

STEP 3

Repeat step 2 in exactly the same way to make a second loop next to the first.

STEP 4

Pass the second loop behind the first without any additional folding or twisting.

STEP 5

Place a pole through the two loops and pull the ends of the rope to tighten the hitch.

STEP 6

When tight, it should look like this.

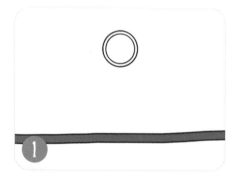

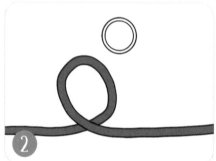

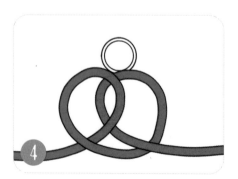

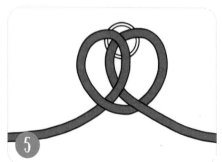

Square lashing

This is used to join two sticks of similar diameter at right angles to each other. You will need about one and a half 'hugs' of cord that is strong enough for the strain it will come under. (One 'hug' is roughly the full span of your arms stretched out.) ³⁄₁₆in (5mm) paracord is good for a huge range of purposes.

STEP 1

Tie a clove hitch around one of the sticks at the point where you want the sticks to be lashed together.

STEP 2

Take the cord up and over the other stick then under the starting stick.

STEP 3

Repeat this pattern – it looks like rucksack straps. The string should make a square shape on both sides of the lashing.

STEP 4

Follow the first lap of the cord and repeat another two times.

STEP 5

Change the direction of the lashing to wrap between the two sticks. This pulls the rucksack straps really tight.

STEP 6

Do this three times then tie the end off with several half hitches (see page 27) onto one of the branches.

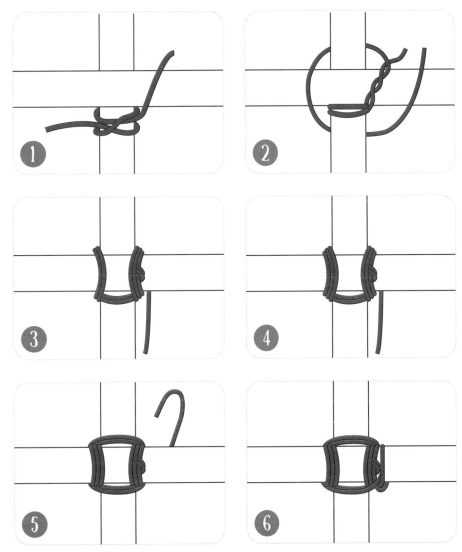

Timber hitch

This is an amazing hitch. Originally used for dragging logs out of woodland, it could be attached to a really heavy tree trunk and dragged a long way using a lot of force and still be really easy to untie at the end. It will be useful in making bows, putting up shelters and taking your log for a walk!

STEP 1

Lay out the pulling part of the rope in line with the log you want to move. This is the standing end.

STEP 2

Turn the working end of the rope at right angles then pass it underneath the log and up the other side.

STEP 3

Pass this end underneath the pulling part.

STEP 4

Bring this end over the pulling part to make a loop.

STEP 5

Twist the working end around itself at least three times. Then pull the pulling part to tighten the hitch. It should grab the log and grip tightly when being dragged around.

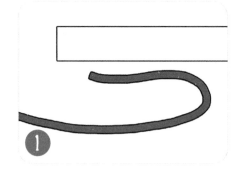

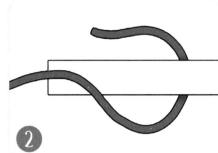

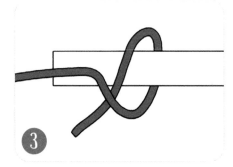

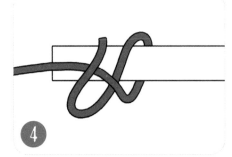

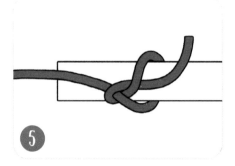

Round turn and two half hitches

I most often use this to tie a line tight onto a tree to make the ridge or guy rope for a tarpaulin or a washing line to dry my soggy socks.

STEP 1

Assuming that the standing end of the rope is attached firmly to something else, perhaps with a timber hitch (see facing page), pull the rope as tight as you can and wrap it at least one full turn around the tree. Keep one hand flat on the turn of rope around the tree to stop it slipping.

STEP 2

Put the working end across the tight line to make a triangle.

STEP 3

Bring the working end up through the triangle and pull tight. This is the first of the two half hitches.

STEP 4

Take the working end back over the taut line to make another loop. It is more like a letter D than a triangle this time.

STEP 5

Again, bring the working end up through the D shape.

STEP 6

Pull tight to make the second half hitch. This should now be very secure and not slip.

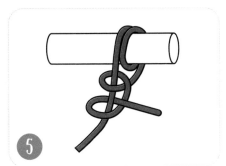

Figure of eight on the bight

This is useful to make a loop in a rope when you want to put up a rope swing.

STEP 1

Grab a long loop of rope (called a bight). We will treat as if it is just a single length of rope. Make a loop with the bight.

STEP 2

Pass the looped end all the way around the two strands of the bight. This will make a double loop.

STEP 3

Wrap the first loop around these strands for one full turn. This makes a second loop under your other hand.

STEP 4

Pull both ends tight to make a strong, secure loop.

Making

Den building

We like to feel at home wherever we are, and an outdoor adventure is no exception. Call it a base, fort, camp, shelter, cubby, camp, wikiup or a bird hide, making some sort of structure from sticks and leaves, tarpaulin and string is hard to resist.

Debris shelters

Building dens with sticks can be done in many different ways from just leaning long sticks against a trunk or horizontal branch. For a free-standing den, the forked stick is your friend.

STEP 1

Find two sturdy forked sticks at least 3ft (1m) in length and a third one that is a bit longer. Lock the three forks together to make a self-supporting tripod. No string should be needed to hold this together.

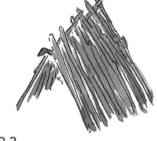

STEP 2

Lean thinner sticks against this frame to make rafters, leaving as small gaps as possible.

STEP 3

Thatch your shelter with leaf litter, starting with a layer of leaves around the base and building it up like bricks.

STEP 4

If you want to stay dry inside when it rains, the thatch will need to be about 12in (30cm) thick and slightly compressed with a few bigger logs on top of it.

STEP 5

It is advisable to lean your weight on the shelter to check that it is sturdy. There will be quite a weight of wood used in the construction and you don't want it to collapse on you once inside. Then all that's left to do is sweep out any leaves on the floor with a broom (see page 92 for how to make one) and move in!

Out for a walk?

If I am walking in the hills or along the coast, I usually take an emergency shelter with me – just in case. These can be great for eating lunch on a wet, cold, windy day and create a cosy feeling of togetherness, boosting everyone's spirits ready for the next part of the walk. They are also sometimes called group shelters, 'Kisu' or bothy bags and can be made or bought for groups as small as two people up to large groups of 12 adults.

Under a tarp

If you're staying in one place for the day, you might want a shelter to keep yourself and your stuff dry, and also to feel at home. A lightweight tarpaulin with guy ropes is ideal and won't take up much room in your bag. The simplest way to put one up is to tie a tight line between two trees using a timber hitch at one end and a round turn and two half hitches at the other (see pages 26–27 for knot instructions). Stretch the corners of the tarp out to make a ridged roof and tie guy lines to nearby trees. The tauter the material is, the easier it will shed rainwater and the less it will flap in the wind.

Making a campfire

A campfire can take any adventure to another level. It allows you to keep warm, see in the dark, cook food and make lots of different things. Lighting a fire with natural materials is some sort of primal urge but it takes practice and skill, and requires some knowledge of the resources around us.

There are lots of possible techniques to light and maintain a fire. This section will explain one fairly straightforward way to make a fire on open ground or in a fire-bowl, as well as the slightly more unusual 'underground rocket stove' for you to experiment with.

Siting your fireplace

- Choose a level site away from the base of trees.
- Avoid lighting on bare rock or on ground with high organic content, such as peat or coniferous woodland soils.
- Make sure you have the landowner's permission to make a fire.
- Check that fires are permitted by local regulations and always respect seasonal/emergency fire bans.

Safety

Below are a few specific pieces of advice that you should heed whenever you're near a fire. This list could go on and on, but just use common sense and stay safe.

- Tie long hair back – burning hair smells awful!
- Kneel, crouch or sit, rather than stand by the fire.
- Keep a big bucket of water close at hand to cool burns or extinguish the fire in an emergency.
- Don't ever use petrol, paraffin or aerosols, etc.
- Make sure that there is no chance of the fire spreading outside your fireplace by removing any surrounding combustible material and storing your firewood supply away from the fire.
- Never leave a smouldering fire. Make sure that all the embers and ground below are cold to the touch before you leave any fire site. If it is a temporary fireplace then clear everything up and leave no trace of your campfire.

Top fire-building tips

Remember the 'six p's': Prior Preparation Prevents Probable Poor Performance. So, take your time, prepare everything you need, and have it easily to hand. It can be boring and frustrating watching someone else trying to light a fire but rushing them will only make it worse!

Collect more tinder than you think you will need. Not having enough dry tinder and kindling will frustrate your attempts to get a good fire going. There are lots of natural materials that can be used as tinder. Birch bark is a great one to start with, but don't be afraid of using cotton wool and newspaper and swapping them for local materials as you practise and learn more about what can be collected and used where you live. There is no such thing as cheating – if you want a fire without getting frustrated, just use what works for you.

It is a good idea to sort several thicknesses of kindling, from matchstick thick to pencil thick.

Only collect dry, dead wood. In dry places it may be possible to collect fallen twigs from the ground but if it has rained, you will need to look for dead twigs that are still attached to trees. Low conifer branches and in the middle of dense holly bushes are good places to look. Some tree species, such as beech, catch fallen twigs from higher in the canopy in their lower branches.

We have ignition!

Learning to rub sticks together to light your fire might be something to aim for, but for now, stick to standard matches (extra-long ones are good for younger children), waterproof matches or a lighter. A fire steel (ferro-magnesium rod) makes showers of very hot sparks that can ignite your tinder. It is well worth getting one for your rucksack – it will provide many challenging hours as you experiment with different tinder.

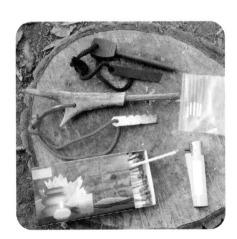

Straightforward campfire

This basic fire can be built on the ground or in a fire bowl. Before you start building your fire, you need to choose a suitable place to light it. It should be flat, away from the base of any trees and have enough room to move around without having to step over the fire.

Clear away any dead leaves or pine needles that might catch and let the fire spread beyond the fireplace. Marking it out with a square of sticks helps define the size of the fire. Avoid edging your fireplace with rocks, as there is a chance that they might explode. You might want to make a bigger square for younger children to keep their knees behind.

STEP 1
Collect your tinder, kindling and main firewood. Lay a few sticks down as a firebase to keep the tinder off damp ground and to allow air to flow under the fire.

STEP 2
Place the tinder bundle on the base.

STEP 3
Divide the finest kindling into two long bundles and place either side of you so that they are easy to hand. Check the wind direction and make sure that it is blowing from behind you. Light the tinder, immediately pick up the kindling bundles and hold them at right angles over the flame. Keep hold of the bundles and move them to get maximum heat from the flames until you hear the wood crackle as it ignites.

STEP 4
Gently place the bundles down and start to add the second size of kindling on top of the flames.

STEP 5
Relax a little and take your time to carefully add more firewood. Resist the urge to poke and prod, as you are more likely to extinguish the flames than get them going.

The underground rocket stove

Sometimes known as the snake hole fire, this can be a very efficient fire to cook on as it uses a relatively little amount of small-diameter firewood and concentrates the heat of the fire on the area at the top of the chimney.

Choose a site very carefully to minimize any negative impact on the plants and animals that live there. Avoid soils with a high organic content – clay soils are ideal. Bare earth on riverbanks can make good spots for rocket stoves.

STEP 1

Clear away any dead leaves or other combustible material and then dig a vertical hole in the top of the bank, about 12in (30cm) from the edge. The diameter of each hole should be at least 4in (10cm).

STEP 2

Dig a horizontal hole into the face of the earth bank, about 12in (30cm) from the top of the slope. Excavate both holes until they join underground at a 90-degree elbow.

STEP 3

Light a fire of small kindling in the entrance to the hole in the bank and when it is established, carefully push it farther into the hole with a long stick. You can then feed the fire from the chimney as well as from the lower opening. When it heats up, it will start to draw air in from the lower hole and hopefully start to roar.

STEP 4

Push a few sticks into the earth around the chimney to make a pot stand. Rest your cooking pot on top and get the dinner on.

Tip

Bark can act like a sponge and store a lot of moisture, so you can increase your chance of success in wet weather by using a thumbnail or the back of a knife to scrape wet bark from your kindling twigs. Alternatively, split a larger piece of firewood through the centre into eighths or sixteenths and carve the driest corner of each slice to make a pile of dry shavings to use as your kindling.

Cooking on sticks

There are various ways to cook over a campfire, but cooking on sticks is very appealing – you don't need to carry pots and pans, you can easily see the food cooking to perfection and there is no washing up! Let's have a look at a few different ways we can use sticks in our campfire kitchen.

Metal fork in wooden handle

Use a palm drill (see page 18) to bore one or two holes in the end of a stick and ram an old fork in the end. Bingo!

Spear stick

Use a knife to whittle (see pages 16–23) the end of a stick into a point. Spear bread to toast or make toffee apples (see page 44).

Basic stick

Use a knife (see page 16) to carefully peel the bark from a non-toxic stick. You can wrap a twist of dough around the peeled end to bake over hot coals. If one end is cooking more quickly, twist the bread from the stick and turn it round until it is a golden brown colour all over and sounds hollow when tapped with a fingernail. Take it off the stick and drizzle honey into the middle for a tasty campfire treat.

Forked branch

When toasting larger slices of bread, a bit more support is needed to stop the toast falling off the stick. If you can find the right stick, an easy fork is made by using a pruning saw to cut a stem with a branch at the end and sharpening both prongs with a knife (see pages 16–23).

Above, left to right: metal fork in wooden handle, spear stick, and forked branch.

Tip

Clean off your cooking sticks to use again and soak in clean water before using them to stop the wood burning as the food cooks.

Basic spit

Sometimes we might want to give our hands a rest or make sure that the food stays exactly the right distance from the heat of the fire. A simple spit will do the job.

STEP 1

Find two forked sticks, cut them to the same length using a pruning saw and sharpen the ends with a knife (see pages 16–23) so that they push into the ground easily.

STEP 2

Push the sticks into the ground on either side of your fire.

STEP 3

Use your knife to peel a green non-toxic stick that is as long as your fireplace is wide.

STEP 4

Push your food onto the green stick and rest it on the forks above the hot coals. Turn the stick occasionally to make sure everything is cooked evenly.

Campfire snacks

Adventurers need energy and there is no better way to get an energy boost than by cooking up a snack on your campfire.

Humans have been preparing and cooking food outdoors for hundreds of thousands of years, and for many people in the world today an open fire is still the only way to cook.

If you are new to it, cooking on the fire can seem tricky but it just takes a little practice to manage the fire to give the right heat at the right time. There are lots of specialized bits of equipment available for campfire cooking but for these recipes, you can leave the pots, pans and tinfoil at home – all you need is the ingredients and a fire. Try these favourites below if you want to have something a bit different from the standard toasted marshmallow.

Tip

Keeping everything clean can be a challenge when cooking outdoors. Remember the same rules for your kitchen at home regarding handling raw meat, keeping food cool and washing hands and utensils well. It's also a good idea to find a stump to keep your food preparation area off the ground, as there are several bacteria occurring in soil that can cause food poisoning.

Toffee apples

You will need
- Apples
- Knife
- Pointed stick
- Brown sugar
- Cinnamon (optional)

STEP 1
These are a sweet treat but not many people can eat a whole one, so core an apple and cut it into eighths. Skewer one section on a pointed stick with the flesh side outwards and the skin towards you. Place it close to the hot coals and turn for a minute or so until the flesh has warmed and softened a little.

STEP 2
Roll the warm apple slice in brown sugar (mix a pinch of cinnamon in if you like the taste) so that it coats the apple.

STEP 3
Re-heat the apple slice on the coals until the sugar melts and caramelizes. Take it away from the heat before it starts to burn. Let it cool before you eat it.

Ash cakes

Cooked directly on hot coals, these simple flatbreads are as ancient as it gets. They work best on a fire that has been burning for a while on dry ground and has a good bed of hot fine ash. Often, people think that this is a dirty way of cooking but the heat of the fire will have killed any germs and the ash just blows off the cooked bread. It really is delicious!

You will need

- Plain flour
- Water
- Pinch of salt
- Stick

STEP 1

Mix together plain flour, water and a pinch of salt until it forms a dough that is stretchy but doesn't stick to your hands. You can add foraged herbs such as wild garlic to give more flavour.

STEP 2

Shape it into flat patties about 4in (10cm) across and ³⁄₁₆in (5mm) thick.

STEP 3

Use a stick to rake out a pile of ash next to the fire and bury the pattie in it, placing a few hot coals on top of the ash.

STEP 4

How long to leave it there is guesswork! It depends on the amount of heat in the ash and the ground but it should be around 10 to 15 minutes – you will have to experiment.

For a more authentic ancient bread, try using spelt flour. If you are feeling really adventurous, find out which wild seeds in your area are safe to use, then collect, winnow and grind them into your own flour.

An egg and bacon banjo

Bacon and egg in a bread roll is the campfire breakfast of champions. Cooked this way, it takes a little while but has the advantage that there is no washing up.

Why the strange name? Because it looks like you are playing an invisible banjo as you wipe the inevitable drips of runny egg yolk from your jumper as you eat!

There are lots of variations on how to hold the bacon near enough the heat for long enough to cook it. We will use a freshly cut (green) stick that is from a non-toxic species.

You will need
- A spit
- Bacon
- Egg
- Pin/nail/tip of sharp knife
- Tongs/heat-proof glove
- Knife or fork
- Bread roll

STEP 1
First you need to make a spit as described on page 43.

STEP 2
Thread the bacon onto the stick like a concertina. You can also just drape several rashers over the stick, but it is more likely that you lose them to the fire or they slide off as they cook. Turn the spit occasionally to cook all sides evenly.

STEP 3
Use a pin, nail or the tip of your knife to carefully drill a ³⁄₁₆in (5mm) hole in the flatter end of the egg without cracking the shell. Make sure that you fully pierce the air sac membrane through to the egg white underneath.

STEP 4
Rake out a pile of hot ash and nestle the egg so that it is nearly buried in the ash with the hole at the top. You can rest hot coals outside the ash if you think it needs more heat. Pull up a log and sit and wait at least 15 minutes for the egg to bake. Don't sit too close as there is always the risk that the egg might explode with a bang if it cooks too quickly!

STEP 5
Use tongs or a heatproof glove to remove the baked egg from the ash. Let it cool a while, then peel the shell from the cooked egg. (This is more difficult to do if your eggs are very fresh.) Mash the peeled egg with a knife or fork into a bread roll then add your bacon and enjoy.

Nature crown

In ancient Persia, Greece and Egypt crowns made of green leaves were worn as a symbol of power or after a victory in battle. Every outdoor adventurer should have their own crown of victory.

To make yours, you can follow the instructions for making a door wreath on page 84 and simply make the hoop the right size to fit on your head. Instead of a bendy branch, you could use reeds or rushes from the water's edge. They can be twisted or plaited together to make them stronger.

Alternatively, stick some double-sided tape onto a strip of card and wrap it round to make a crown. It might need extra tape or staples to stop it from coming undone. Then you can decorate your cardboard crown by sticking things to it that you've found on a nature walk. Be sure to pick only things that are very common and safe to use. Make sure whatever you attach to the tape is dry or it will fall off.

Bow and arrow

So, you want to be Katniss Everdeen, Legolas or Robin Hood! You are going to need a bow and to learn to shoot it.

Archery is an ancient skill that has been practised across the globe for millennia. It has developed from a way of hunting game with deceptively simple stick-bows to modern Olympic archery with high-tech, expensive bows with sights, stabilizers and lots of other gadgets. Lots of fun can be had with a green stick and a piece of string but it must always be remembered that even a primitive, low-powered bow is a weapon and should be treated respectfully and used safely.

You will need

- Knife (see page 16)
- Archer's-height thumb-thick green stick
- ³⁄₆₄in (1mm) cotton string/fishing line
- ³⁄₈in (1cm) diameter straight, long stick
- Feathers and glue or duct tape

Making the bow

To make the simplest of bows, cut a thumb-thick green stick that is nearly as tall as the person who is going to shoot it. It needs to be not too bendy, not too stiff and not brittle. Brace one end on the ground against the inside of one foot, hold the top steady and push the middle of the stick to see how much it will bend. There is a saying that a bow is just a stick that is nine-tenths broken – we need to make sure that it doesn't go that last tenth as we make and use it.

STEP 1

Cut a notch about ¾in (2cm) from each end of the stick. The notch should be at a slight angle downwards towards the handle of the bow.

STEP 2

Make your bowstring. This needs to be strong enough not to break when you draw and release an arrow. For a thin bow for a small child, ³⁄₆₄in (1mm) cotton string may be strong enough or you can use a suitable thickness of fishing line. Archers change bowstrings fairly frequently, so if you know someone who does archery, see if they have any old strings you could re-purpose. Several strands of thinner string can be laid beside each other and twisted together to make a strong bow string. Tie your string onto the notch at one end of the bow with a timber hitch (see page 26).

STEP 3

Bend the bow, as described earlier, and tie the other end with a round turn and two half hitches (see page 27) so that the gap between the string and the bow is the same as the archer's fist with thumb outstretched. Test the string by pulling it back and forward without letting go to make sure that the knots are well seated and the string is securely held.

Tip

If you want your bow to last
a little bit longer then peel the
bark off and let it dry before
stringing and drawing it.
Removing the string between
shooting sessions will stop
your bow taking on a curved
shape permanently and losing
power over time.

Arrow making

Hunt for the longest, straightest, branch-free stems you can find. Dense hedgerows that haven't been cut for a couple of years are good places to look. They should be around ⅜in (1cm) in diameter and as long as the archer's neck to fingertip.

STEP 1

One end of the stick will be slightly thicker than the other. This will be the pointy end so you can sharpen it with a knife or char it over the fire and rub it on a rock to get the right shape.

STEP 2

Carefully use a knife to cut a v-shaped groove called a 'nock' in the other end of the arrow.

STEP 3

Arrows can be shot bare shafted but will look – and more importantly – fly better if they have feathers called 'fletchings' at the back. If you can find feathers, they can be cut to shape and glued on or you can improvise with duct tape.

Shooting

- Make sure that you have a clear space to shoot where there is no chance of anyone wandering into your shooting area. Never point a nocked arrow at anyone, even as a joke.

- Stand side on to your target with your feet shoulder width apart. Put your arrow nock in the middle of the string on the outside of the bow so that it rests on the back of the hand gripping the bow. Grip the string with one finger above the arrow and two below. The nock should hold the arrow on the string.

- Draw the string back to your face and relax your string fingers to release the arrow. Watch it fly.

- This is addictive and as you practise, your shooting will improve. There is a lifetime's worth of research, experimentation and enjoyment in primitive archery and it is unlikely that your first bow will be your last.

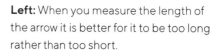

Left: When you measure the length of the arrow it is better for it to be too long rather than too short.

Rope swing

A rope swing hanging from a tree in the woods or over a river can be hard to resist. The thrill of flying and spinning through the air appeals to all ages. Swinging on vines isn't usually an option, so how do you go about making your own rope swing that you can take home at the end of the day and make again somewhere else?

First, find a tree with a suitable, strong, overhanging branch where the ground is clear to swing so you won't bash into anything. Some species are stronger than others, so find out if there are any species that are best avoided in your area. Steer clear of any tree that is obviously dead or dying. Check the shape of the tree – branch unions closer to right angles to the trunk can be stronger than tight forks.

Check the fall zone. Ask yourself what might happen if you fall off or the branch or rope fails. Where would I land? How far might I fall? What would I land on? Would anything land on me? There are no right answers to those questions but it would be wise to think about them in advance to help decide if this is a good spot for a swing or not.

Make sure that the rope is at least three times as long as the distance from the branch to the ground. Your tree may be climbable but often the rope will be higher than you might want to climb. Throwing the rope is usually a better option.

You will need
- Approx. 65ft (20m) of strong rope
- Sturdy stick for a seat

STEP 1

Hold the rope in one hand, slide your other hand along and bring back to form a loop. Rolling the rope between finger and thumb will help the rope form a clean loop rather than a figure of eight shape. Repeat three times.

STEP 2

Wrap around the three loops once to divide the loops into a top and bottom part.

STEP 3

Take a loop of rope and pass through the top part. Hold this coil in one hand.

STEP 4

Gather a coil of three larger loops of rope in the other hand and make sure that the remainder of the rope is not tangled, snagged on any debris or loose around your own feet.

STEP 5

Throw the small coil underarm over the branch, then immediately throw the second larger coil after it so that it has its own momentum and doesn't drag the small coil back. The small coil should fall apart when it descends over the branch.

STEP 6

Reach up and grab a loop of the longer side of the rope (not the end that was thrown over the branch) and tie an overhand or figure of eight knot in the rope.

STEP 7

Thread the short end (this is where the swing seat will go) through the eye of the knot and pull down to slide the knot up to meet the branch. Pull tight and test with full body weight.

STEP 8

Tidy the non-swinging part of the rope out of the way so that it can't get tangled up in the swing. Tie a seat stick onto the base, using a round turn and two half hitches (see page 27) then have fun!

When it is time to go, you can retrieve the swing by first untying the seat then pulling the non-swinging end of the rope to move the knot downwards and free of the swinging end. The rope will feed over the branch and land on the ground. Mind your head!

Little boats

Messing about in the water is irresistible. There is something about the sounds of moving water, the feel of it on your bare feet and trying to direct and channel it that has a magnetic pull. Building little boats to float on still or moving water will test your engineering skills and allow your imagination to go wild.

Folded soft rush boats

These are super-quick and easy to make. On still water, it is fun to race boats with the wind behind them. In a stream you can see which survives the rapids.

You will need

- Rush stem
- Scissors/knife (see page 16)
- Leaf

STEP 1

Cut a single stem of the rush with a knife or scissors and fold it around four times to make a hull about 4in (10cm) long.

STEP 2

Halfway along the last fold, bend the rush at 90 degrees and wrap it around the hull three times. Make sure that you double back to secure the long folds of the hull and stop them unravelling.

STEP 3

Take the tip of the rush and thread it through the middle of the hull to lock the wrapping off and make the mast of the boat.

STEP 4

Thread a leaf onto the mast to make a sail.

STEP 5

Experiment with tall and short masts and large and small sails.

Left: Lots of natural materials are great for boat building. One favourite that is found on every continent except Antarctica is the Juncus family of rushes.

On one camping trip the kids spent about two hours making boats and put them in a little harbour behind a rock in a stream. When the harbour was full, the boats were released and followed downstream with the aid of a long stick to rescue those that got stuck on the bank.

Bundle rush boats

In 1969 and 1970, Norwegian archaeologist and explorer Thor Heyerdahl built boats from papyrus and successfully sailed the Ra II across the Atlantic Ocean from Morocco to Barbados. Papyrus is a sedge rather than a reed so you might try different plants for this design of boat. To tell the difference, try to remember the old botanists saying that 'sedges have edges and rushes are round'.

You will need
- Sedges or rushes
- Scissors/knife (see page 16)
- String
- Stick

STEP 1
Cut a handful-sized bundle of sedges or rushes with a knife or scissors.

STEP 2
Tie string tightly around each end so that the bundle stays together.

STEP 3
Trim the ends of the bundle into a bow and stern shape.

STEP 4
Add a stick in the middle as a spacer so that there is room for your passengers.

STEP 5
Add some passengers (acorns, stick people or jelly sweets!) and see if they stay dry on their journey downstream.

Twig boats

As long as it floats it can be a boat. From a punky (rotted) branch with a leaf sail to an intricately tied raft, no two twig boats are ever the same. Pictured below are a few ideas.

Why not set your boats afloat with gum and jelly sweets or pine-cone passengers? Will they stay dry? Whose boat can go farthest or fastest?

Below, top left to right: Jelly sweet passengers, pine-cone passengers, wood-offcut Viking boat with paper sail.
Below, bottom left to right: Punky branch boat, lashed raft.

Tip

You may not always retrieve your boats, so make sure the materials and passengers are biodegradable and won't become rubbish wherever they end up.

Natural paints

The oldest paintings in the world are between 60,000 and 40,000 years old and can be found in France, Spain, Indonesia and Australia. They were painted on rocks with ground-up earth, charcoal and burnt bones. Their meanings have often been lost but we can still admire them as art that often took great skill to make.

We can use the same materials and techniques to make our own natural paints but finding a wide range of colours may take a good bit of exploring. The coloured powders used to make paints are called pigments. The soil at the surface often has lots of dead organic matter in it, which you can smudge on a page but doesn't make great paint. You may need to dig a little and can often find different colours in one hole as you dig deeper. Sometimes the colour of wet soil or clay changes dramatically when it is exposed to air and dries.

Tip

Try drying some leaves or petals and crushing them into dust to make a wider range of pigment colours.

You will need

- A trowel or small spade to dig down to the sub-soil
- Some containers to keep your pigments in
- A mortar and pestle to grind them up
- A sieve to separate the finest dust, which you want to keep
- Something to bind the pigments together so that they stick to whatever you paint them on

STEP 1

Dry the soil in the hot sun, beside a fire or even in the oven at home.

STEP 2

Grind it up with a mortar and pestle to a fine dust.

STEP 3

Sieve to remove any larger pieces.

STEP 4

Mix the finely ground pigment with a binder (also called a medium) and get painting with one of your new brushes (see page 66).

Using egg as a binder

Egg tempera is a very old paint that dries quickly to a matt finish. Once it is dry it lasts a long time and you can paint over it.

- Crack an egg and separate the yolk and the white.
- Put the yolk in a screw top jar with a tablespoon of water and shake vigorously with the lid on.
- Add some pigment powder until you have the colour that you want.

Milk paint

This paint gives a lovely worn look on wooden items.

- Mix 4 parts milk powder, 1 part bicarbonate of soda, 1 part pigment, 6 parts cold water and let sit for an hour before using.

Alternatively, you can use white PVA glue to mix with a drop of water and your pigment.

Natural paintbrushes

You have seen how to make natural paints from earth on page 64, now you need ways to paint with them. It is an endless experiment trying out different natural objects with types of paint to give different effects.

Try hammering the end of a green stick onto a firm surface until the fibres separate and become like a brush. It will probably take a few tries to work out how hard to bash it to get a good result.

Collect anything that might hold paint and has enough give to apply the paint to the surface. Many coniferous trees as well as woody herbs such as lavender and rosemary make interesting marks. Tie bundles to a stick with string or elastic bands.

Just use a feather. What about the other end of your quill? See page 70.

As well as making brushes, try printing with natural objects by dipping them in paint and pressing down or even rolling things like pine cones across the surface.

What to paint on to?

If your paint is completely natural and is going to wash away within a day or two then you can paint on just about anything as long as it will quickly leave no trace. Of course, you might want to keep your artwork and take it home. A sketchbook kept for messy outdoor painting could be good. Old fabric, chunks of dry firewood, sections of old bark and sides of cardboard boxes are all good surfaces to paint on outdoors. Like with most things, experiment and you will find all sorts of great effects with different materials.

Forest friends

Tree spirits, fairies, pixies, piskies, boggarts, puppets, dolls, forest friends, whatever you call them, the little people are everywhere in the woods. Make your own to act out stories, live in a tiny house or just pop them in the trees to spook random passers-by.

You will need

- Thumb-thick branch
- Knife (see page 16)
- Various natural materials – leaves, feathers, flowers, etc.
- String

STEP 1

Find or cut a thumb-thick branch about 12in (30cm) long.

STEP 2

Whittle the bark from one end (see pages 16–23) and draw on a face.

STEP 3

Collect up some abundant natural materials to dress up your forest friend and tie on with string.

STEP 4

If you like, before you dress it, you can tie arms on to your one-stick forest friend with a square lashing (see page 25).

STEP 5

Find your forest friend a place to live outside. Maybe they will want to stay in hiding or perhaps be found by other inquisitive adventurers.

Tree protector

If you go to a tree planting event, why not leave a forest friend with your tree as a sort of scarecrow (or scare rabbit / scare vole / scare deer) to look after the sapling? Newly planted trees have a lot to contend with and need care if they are going to survive. As the stick person rots into the soil, its nutrients will be taken back up into the young tree and recycled – becoming part of another tree.

Above: Search carefully and you might find a wonky stick with legs and arms that you can cut to look like a stick person.
Left: If you take your forest friend home, you can dress it up with some scrap materials for funky evening wear.

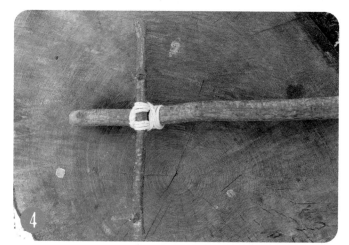

Wassail

When meeting or leaving a forest friend, greet with a wassail. Wassail is an old Anglo Saxon greeting meaning 'good health to you'. Wassail ceremonies take place in orchards around the UK in early January to scare off evil spirits, bless the apple trees and ensure a good crop of fruit later in the year. Make sure you yell 'wassail' as loudly as you can!

Feather quill

To make your own medieval pen you will need to find a big sturdy feather at least 8in (20cm) long so that it is strong enough not to bend and won't scratch the paper. Search for large gull feathers on the coast or ask a farmer for some goose or turkey feathers in December. If you can't find any, you can always buy some from a craft supply shop.

Just like your fingernails and hair, feathers are made of a material called keratin. If you hold the feather up to the light, you will see that the tip of the feather is solid and will need to be cut away to allow your ink into the hollow tube of the quill.

You will need
- Knife (see page 16)
- Large feather, e.g. gull, turkey or goose

STEP 1
Using your knife, scrape and smooth the lower feathers from the shaft of the feather so that you have enough room to hold it.

STEP 2
Cut the tip off the feather at 45 degrees. Remove any loose material inside the tube of the quill.

STEP 3
Square off the point of this diagonal cut.

STEP 4
Cut a slit in the long part of the quill. As you press down on the paper, the split opens slightly and lets more ink flow onto the nib.

STEP 5
Taper the sides of the cut to form a thinner nib for the pen.

STEP 6
Shape the tip of the nib to be pointed, square or angled, depending on the writing or drawing style you want to use.

Tip

It is important that your knife is small and sharp so that you can make clean cuts.

Now it is time to try writing a nature poem (see page 116) with your homemade ink (see page 72).

Natural inks

You can have lots of fun writing messages for friends using the feather quill on page 70 and these natural inks. There's even a super-easy invisible ink for secret messages.

Berry inks

You will need
- Ripe berry fruit
- Fork/spoon for mashing
- Old cloth/sieve
- Jar
- Rubber gloves

For a simple natural ink, collect some ripe berry fruit and mash it up. Some berries might need to be cooked for a while to soften them enough to mash but don't add any water to the fruit as you will end up with very diluted colours. Strain it through some old cloth or a sieve into a jar and get writing. It is a good idea to wear rubber gloves unless you want to have ink-stained hands.

Oak gall ink

You will need
- Dry brown oak apples, about 2oz (50g)
- Mortar and pestle
- Water, about 18fl oz (500ml)
- Pan for boiling water (optional)
- Containers x 2
- Steel wool/rusty nails/old bits of iron
- Water/vinegar
- Sieve

This is the stuff that monks used to write illustrated manuscripts with and can last for hundreds of years. The main ingredient for the ink is the oak apple, which is a gall or growth caused by a tiny wasp which lays its eggs in a leaf bud. The larvae develop inside the gall and then eat their way out leaving a tiny exit hole.

They can be found on the tree in spring and summer but by collecting from the ground you can be sure that the wasp has left the gall and you won't be harming anything when you grind them up.

STEP 1
Break up a about 2oz (50g) of dry brown oak apples, then grind them in a mortar and pestle.

STEP 2
Soak the ground galls in about 18fl oz (500ml) of water overnight, or longer if possible. Soaking them in water gives a lovely brown colour that won't fade too quickly. To speed the process up, boil up the galls in the water for half an hour.

STEP 3
Soak some steel wool, rusty nails or old bits of iron for a week or so in just enough water or vinegar to cover.

STEP 4
Strain both of the mixtures and combine them.

STEP 5
We can use this mixture to make jet-black ink. The iron reacts chemically with the tannin in the galls and causes a dramatic colour change. Over hundreds of years, as the iron in the ink oxidizes, the ink becomes brown.

Invisible ink

You will need
- Lemon
- Container
- Candle/fire embers

For invisible ink, simply squeeze the juice of a lemon into a container and use a feather quill to write a message onto paper with the juice. Let it dry. You won't be able to read it easily until you pass the paper over heat for the message to be revealed. Take care not to set your message on fire – use a candle or the embers of a fire and hold the paper just close enough to see the colour change.

Nature diary

As you get to know a place throughout the seasons, it's a great idea to record what you notice in a nature diary. You could use a ready-made notebook but it is much more fun to make your own. Pack your diary in your adventuring bag so that you can write and remember all the interesting things that you see when you are out and about.

You will need

- Paper
- Length of wood the same size as your paper
- Knife (see page 16)
- Drill (see page 18)
- Card/stiff paper, slightly larger than your paper
- Hole punch
- String

STEP 1

Cut a length of wood the same size as the width of your paper.

STEP 2

Drill (see page 22) two holes right the way through the wood.

STEP 3

Baton (see page 22) the wood with a knife to split it into two halves.

STEP 4

Punch holes in your paper and card to line up with the holes in the wood.

STEP 5

Thread string through the holes and tie tight to bind your notebook.

Tip

You might need to fold or score the card lightly at the binding to make it easier to open.

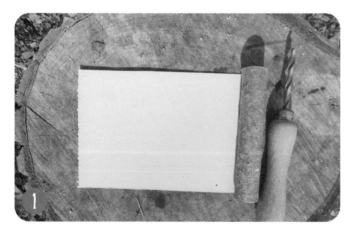

Mandala leaf art

Making art in nature involves slowing down, taking notice of the natural world around you and focusing on patterns. Why not create something beautiful to leave behind for others to discover and wonder at, like a giant mandala?

Mandala is a Sanskrit word that means circle and these geometric circle diagrams represented the universe to Hindus and Buddhists in India. Monks still spend days making them from powdered chalk as a sort of meditation. You will see how easy it is to get lost in the making and leave everyday stresses and worries behind.

Use eight straight sticks to make the spokes of a wheel and edge the rim of the wheel with lots more shorter sticks. Divide each section into smaller parts and fill each part with contrasting materials or smaller patterns. Rings of circle patterns and spirals can all be equally effective. Symmetry can be visually appealing but free-form designs without restrictions will really let individual creativity flourish.

मण्डल

Above: Sanskrit for 'mandala'.

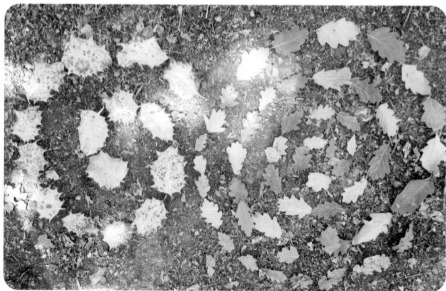

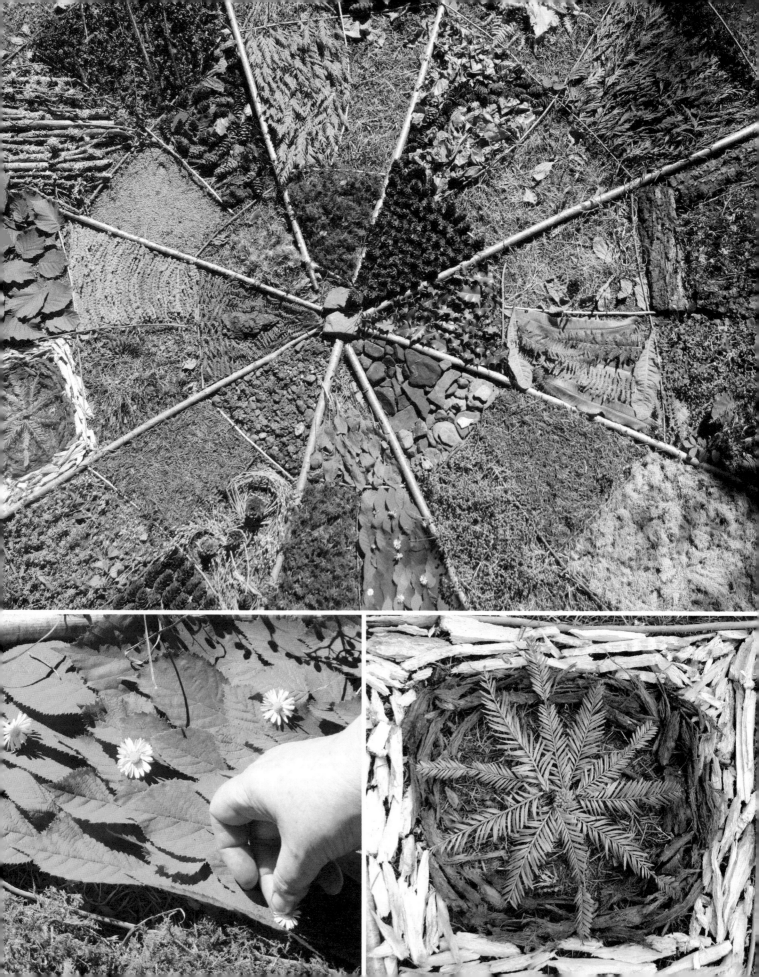

Walking stick

Whether you want a staff like Gandalf or just some help walking up steep hills, a walking stick can be useful for any big adventure. You may be lucky and find a good walking stick lying around and it might even be worth taking home and keeping.

If you want a straight stick (this is best for carving), then you might need to take a saw and cut one. (See pages 16–23 for advice on knives, saws and carving techniques.) It should be about chest height, but cut it a bit longer as it is much easier to saw some wood off than to add some on! Remember, you need to have permission to use the saw and from whoever looks after the land – check page 22 for advice on pruning branches.

Q: When is the best time to cut a walking stick?
A: Whenever you see it.

In the spring, the bark will peel off easily, so you may need to let it dry for a week or two if you want to carve patterns in the bark. Spirals, rings and crisscross patterns look good and can be made with the stop cut and thumb push cuts shown on page 23.

Carve the handle of your stick so that it works well for walking. It can be good to have a smooth section that will slide through your hand, a textured bit with a grip pattern and a rounded top.

You can carve the stick all at once or bit by bit on your journeys as a reminder of where you went and what you did. In the Alps, it is still possible to buy little metal badges in mountain huts to nail onto a wooden stick to record where you have been.

To attach a wrist cord, drill a hole (see page 22) near the top of the stick and whittle away any stringy wood from the edges. Thread and tie some paracord, boot lace or old leather to make a long wrist loop.

Another style of walking stick has a forked branch at the top and is called a thumb stick. Try to find a wide fork with fairly equal-sized branches and cut it to size. You might need to carve the fork a little to get a good shape for your thumb.

Twig picture frame

Frame a view of a beautiful landscape, a close-up of some moss or a painting you've created using natural paints and paintbrushes. A simple picture frame can be made with four sticks lashed together in a square or rectangle.

Find your sticks – straight, regular, wonky, it doesn't matter. Lay out the frame shape and, using string, tie a square lashing at each corner. (Check page 25 for instructions on how to do a square lashing.) By the fourth one, you will have mastered it. Leave any extra string dangling – it may be useful to hang your frame up.

If you are walking along a narrow path with a group of people, use your frames to put around interesting things such as animal tracks or flowers so that the people behind you don't miss out or stand on them.

Live vlog to WoodTube through your frame.

Choose a view and prop or hang your frame to show it. It could be a landscape, an object or a close-up. You might want to choose a spot for viewers to stand and see exactly what you have chosen.

Rest your frame on the mantelpiece or a shelf at home. You can use it to frame photos of your adventures.

Nature wand

Every stick can be a wand and every wand has its own built-in spell, but how do you make your wand your own and release the magic? As the saying goes – the wand chooses the wizard. So, when you have been chosen by a stick in the forest, you need to personalize it with some carving or other decoration so that it stays yours forever.

There are many options for customizing your wand by carving it with a whittling knife (see pages 16–23).

If you can easily drill a hole in the end of the stick (see page 22), why not add a core of something magical like a Phoenix feather or Thestral hair and seal the end with a wooden plug?

If you can identify what type of tree your wand came from, try and find out its scientific name. These usually come from Latin and, if spoken with enough flourish, often make excellent spells.

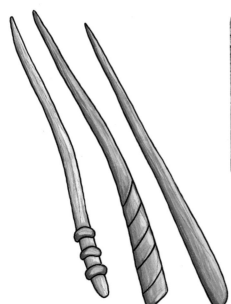

You could remove the bark apart from on the handle.

Use stop and thumb push cuts (see page 22) to make spiral or stripe patterns in the wood or on the bark.

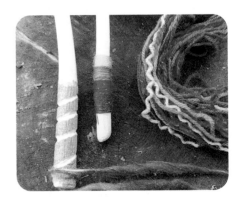

Decorate your wand with some natural paint (see page 64).

Use wool to add even more colour.

Door wreath

All over the world, people place woven circles of twigs and leaves on their doors, monuments and special places at particular times. These have different meanings in different places. Sometimes they are to bless or protect a place, others are symbols of remembrance, power, or victory in battle. Wreaths of olive branches cut from one sacred olive tree were awarded to the winners of the ancient Olympic Games in Greece.

People often make a circle of green winter leaves to mark the midwinter festival of Yule or Christmas. Why not make one to hang on your door to mark the festive season? The word wreath comes from the old English 'wriðan' which meant 'to twist or bend' and that gives us a big clue as to what we need to do to make one.

You will need

- A straight green shoot from a pliable tree such as hazel or willow – as long as possible and at least 5ft (1.5m)
- Secateurs/big scissors
- String/garden wire

STEP 1

Train the wood to bend by gently flexing it away from you with your thumbs.

STEP 2

Repeat and increase the amount of bending until you can form the middle of the branch into a hoop without kinking. Keep weaving the ends around the hoop. It can be any size you like but 12in (30cm) across is a good size to aim for.

STEP 3

Twist the two ends around the original hoop to strengthen it and tuck them in so that it can't unwind. You might want to tie it together with a piece of string or garden wire to stop it unravelling.

STEP 4

Cut thin evergreen branches with secateurs or big scissors. Twist and weave them into the gaps in the hoop and tie on with string or wire if you need to.

STEP 5

Build the wreath up until you can't see the hoop any more, then attach a hanging string and put it on your door.

Woodblock stamps

Create the same pattern again and again with a custom-designed wooden printing block. You can make your printing blocks by using a palm drill to bore a pattern of holes in the end of a length of wood.

You will need

- A round length of wood at least 2¾in (7cm) in diameter that is long enough to hold safely while sawing
- Sawhorse/vice/crook of tree
- A pruning saw (see page 16)
- Pencil/charcoal
- Drill (see page 18)
- Knife (optional, see page 16)

STEP 1

Place your round of wood firmly in a sawhorse, vice or the crook of tree. Saw the end off the round (see page 22) to make it as flat as possible. This is important if you want all of the pattern to show when you print with it.

STEP 2

Mark out your pattern with a pencil or some charcoal.

STEP 3

Drill holes (see page 22) to remove wood from the pattern – these are the white spaces in your design.

STEP 4

Saw off a 4in (10cm) section with the pattern at one end. Your block is now ready to use but if you like, you can carve the top of the stamp into a shape that is more comfortable to hold.

STEP 5

Experiment with printing. If you are impatient then dipping your stamp in a muddy puddle might give you enough colour to test out how the block prints. Alternatively, mix up some natural paint or ink (see pages 64 and 72) and apply to the raised areas of the block. You can repeat print on fabric, make greetings cards, gift tags or personalize your own possessions.

Tip

You might find that placing the paper or material onto something like a mouse mat gives a better result than a hard worktop or table. Experiment to discover what works best for you.

Above: Complex designs are cut into hardwood with chisels and knives to make printing blocks for fabric in parts of India.

Tip

Seasoned wood will be harder to drill than green wood, but will give a crisper pattern when it comes to printing.

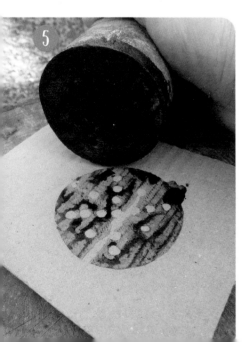

Wind chimes

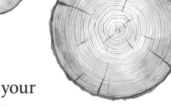

Hang these wind chimes at your outdoor camp or at the door of your home for some (hopefully) relaxing natural sounds in the gentle breeze.

Round chimes

You will need
- Dry, hard wood branch
- Pruning saw (see page 16)
- Drill (see page 18)
- String

STEP 1
Using a pruning saw, cut some ²⁵⁄₆₄in (1cm) thick slices from a dry, hard wood branch (see page 22). Drill a hole in each (see page 22) and tie a 12in (30cm) length of string through the hole.

STEP 2
Tie each slice to a branch, arranging them like steps so that each one will hit against those either side of it when the wind blows. Test in different-strength winds to see if the slices need to be heavier or lighter to work best.

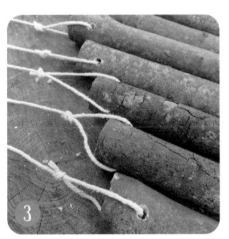

Stick chimes

You will need

- 2 sticks
- String
- Different lengths of dried wood
- Pruning saw (see page 16)
- Natural paints (optional, see page 64)
- Drill (see page 18)
- Big disc of wood/large pebble

STEP 1

Start with two sticks joined with a square lashing (see page 25) to make a cross. We will hang the chimes from this like a puppet.

STEP 2

Test different lengths of dried wood to see what sort of noises they make when they knock into each other. Choose six to eight of them and saw (see page 22) to different lengths for a variety of tones.

STEP 3

Drill a hole in the top of each one and tie a length of string through the hole.

STEP 4

Tie one or two near to the centre of the cross so that they are close to each other but not touching when it is still. Tie something heavy, such as a big disc of wood or a large pebble, to hang from the middle of the cross. This will weigh the wind chime down and hold it steady as well as bash into the chimes to make a better sound.

Smelly potions

Exploring using all of our senses lets us find all sorts of things that we normally would never notice. Some smells in nature, such as a forest of wild garlic, a hedgerow of summer wildflowers or even a dead deer, are really strong and obvious. Others are hidden away and need to be unlocked by making a smelly potion. All you need is an old cup or pot, a little water and a mixing stick.

Pick small amounts of plants and test if they are ingredients you want to use by crushing between your fingers and smelling closely. Perhaps you want to make something that smells beautiful and enchanting or something vile to make people retch. Choose your ingredients carefully to get the right balance of aromas and make sure to keep squashing all the ingredients with your mixing stick for maximum smelliness. Be careful with very smelly plants where even a tiny amount can overwhelm a potion.

When you think the potion is ready, add a little magical spring water to activate the full powers of the potion. Give your mixture a name and see what other people think of it. Can they guess any of the ingredients from the smell?

Finally, raise your glass to the plants that made it and give a loud wassail (see page 69).

Remember, don't drink your magic potion – it's just for smelling!

Broomstick

The besom broom made of a bundle of birch twigs is the typical witches' broomstick, and they are still used for brushing up leaves across Europe today. The making of real besom brooms is an endangered craft and they are only made in the traditional way by a handful of people. Ours won't be up to that standard but will be perfect for a game of Quidditch or casting the odd spell.

To make your own Nimbus 2000 you will need:

- A bundle of natural material for the head of the broom. Traditionally birch twigs are used, but just use what you can find – long grass straw, reeds, or long thin twigs from other trees or bushes (if you want your broom to last, these need to be well dried before you do the next stage)
- String/garden wire
- Pliers
- Pruning saw (see page 16)
- A suitable stick for a handle, about 3ft (1m) long
- Knife (see page 16)
- Hammer
- Nail

STEP 1

The difficult bit is compressing the bundle of twigs and holding them tight enough to tie into a tight bundle. Bind them really tightly with string tied securely or garden wire twisted tightly with a pair of pliers. Depending on the size of your broom, you might need to secure the twigs at two different points, as in the photograph.

STEP 2

With your bundle of twigs firmly on a saw horse, saw the twigs at one end (see page 22).

STEP 3

Take the stick you will use as a handle and sharpen with a knife (see pages 20–23).

STEP 4

Ram the sharpened stick into the bundle of twigs by holding the brush part and firmly tapping the other end onto a hard surface.

STEP 5

To keep the handle from slipping, hammer a nail through the twigs into the handle.

Campfire beads

People have been shaping the earth under their feet into useful and beautiful things for about 30,000 years. Pottery allowed people to store extra food and move from hunting and gathering to settling down and starting farming.

Clay objects need to be fired in a hot fire or kiln to harden and stop them dissolving back into the earth. There are lots of complicated ways to do this, but, luckily for us, some really simple ways can work as well.

To make your own 'primitive' pottery beads you'll need some clay. If you are lucky, you might be able to dig up some clay near where you live. I collect my local clay from eroded riverbanks but have also asked a friendly farmer for some that was turned over by a plough.

With freshly dug clay you will need to pick out any stones and roots and test that it keeps whatever shape you make it into. If you are stuck, you can buy a bag of potters' clay but avoid using air-drying clay for this project because it often contains plastic fibres to prevent cracking.

You will need
- Clay
- Metal tent peg/smooth, even twig
- String
- Campfire
- Metal peg
- Fire gloves/tongs/long forked sticks
- Plenty of dry firewood

STEP 1
Work a small piece of clay in your hands until it has no lumps and will roll into a smooth ball with no cracks.

STEP 2
Use a metal tent peg or a smooth, even twig to make a neat hole through the middle of the ball of clay. Try not to squash it as you push the peg in!

Tip
This fire will be bigger than a normal campfire, so make sure that there is no chance of it spreading or damaging nearby trees or shelters.

STEP 3

Leave the bead smooth or decorate it with patterns scratched or poked in the surface using the end of the peg or twig.

STEP 4

Make a few to fill your necklace plus a few spares in case some of the beads don't make it through the firing process.

STEP 5

Let the beads dry for a few days until the clay is a paler colour.

STEP 6

Place your beads in, or on, the hot embers in the middle of a fire (see pages 36–41 for advice on making a fire) and let them warm up slowly. You can experiment with ways of letting the heat get to all parts of the beads evenly. One way is to put them on a metal peg and to suspend it above the embers. Fire gloves, tongs or long forked sticks are essential to protect your hands from the heat of the fire.

STEP 7

Carefully build a dome of dry firewood over the beads.

STEP 8

Fan the fire until it catches and add firewood as needed to keep the fire burning hot for at least half an hour.

STEP 9

You might be able to see the beads within the fire. When hot enough they should be glowing red. It is time to leave the fire completely alone until it has died right down and the beads are slowly cooling.

STEP 10

Remove the beads from the embers with fire gloves, tongs or long forked sticks.

STEP 11

When cooled, wash any ash off then thread them on a string to wear for those special woodland occasions.

Houses for little people

Sometimes you don't need to move very much at all to have an adventure. If you come across somewhere that the little people might like to live, you may want to make life a bit more comfortable for them. Good places to build can often be found in the buttress roots of trees, crumbling riverbanks, big rocks, and on sandy, stony and rocky beaches.

Little rope ladder

If you want to help the hidden folk climb up to another level, why not make them a rope ladder?

You will need
- A piece of string
- As many small strong sticks as you want to have rungs on your ladder

STEP 1
Find the middle of the string. This will be the top of the ladder. Tie a double figure of eight knot (see page 28) to make a loop.

STEP 2
Lay one stick across the strings and tie it onto each strand with a clove hitch (see page 24).

STEP 3
Repeat as many times as you need to for your ladder to reach where you want it to go.

The 'hidden people'

In Iceland today it is said that over half the population believe in the *huldufólk* or hidden folk who live just like us but hidden away in large rocks. Sometimes houses and hotels are even built around big boulders and roads are diverted, rather than blasting the rocks and disturbing the hidden people. People tell stories of the *huldufólk* helping people in need as well as breaking machinery or causing accidents when they are upset. If such people did exist, are there any special places where might they live in your neighbourhood?

Pencil holder

A hedgehog-shaped pencil holder is a fun and useful thing to make. You'll need to learn a few skills and have some tools to hand – you'll find the information on pages 16–23.

You will need

- Straight, dry log without knots that will split cleanly in half
- Knife (see page 16)
- Palm drill (see page 18)
- Pruning saw (see page 16)
- Paints/pens

STEP 1
Cut the log longer than the final piece so that you can hold it more easily when drilling.

STEP 2
Use your knife to baton (see page 22) and split the log then choose which half you want to use.

STEP 3
Use a knife to whittle one end of the stick nearly to a point (see pages 20–23). This will be the hedgehog's face.

STEP 4
You will need to drill quite a few $5/16$–$3/8$in (8–10mm) holes, so make a large-sized palm drill (see page 18). Be extra careful using these tools and make sure you get adult permission and assistance.

STEP 5
Drill enough holes for all your pencils. They should be at right angles to the surface of the wood. Carefully cut the wood to size.

STEP 6
Paint or draw a face on your hedgehog pencil holder then load it up with all your pencils or pens.

Leaf bashing

Sometimes called 'Hapa Zome', leaf bashing is a great way to make long-lasting, intricate prints of plant leaves on fabric. It is a hands-on way to learn about the properties of different plants, and to notice their shapes and structures in real detail.

Leaves that are not too hard or waxy work well, and some species will produce good results in the spring but not later in the year when their leaves have become harder.

For material to print on, old cotton bed sheets work very well as does calico, which is cheap and easily available in fabric shops.

You will need
- A variety of leaves
- Cotton or calico material
- Piece of card (optional)
- Rubber mallet/pebble/round of wood

STEP 1
Pick a few interesting leaves and arrange them on the material you wish to print on. Place the material on a hard, smooth surface like a plank of wood, paving slab or tree trunk. Any patterns, like tree rings, on the surface that you hammer on might be visible in the final print.

STEP 2
Place a piece of card over the top to make a leaf sandwich or fold spare material over the top to make a mirrored print.

STEP 3
Beat the leaf sandwich with something flat and heavy. A rubber mallet is ideal but a big pebble or round of wood can also work. This is the fun bit, especially if you have had a taxing morning and want to let off steam!

STEP 4
Take away the covering, peel any leaf fragments from the material and admire the patterns you have made.

Tip
Look out for your fingers on your free hand and keep them out of the bashing zone!

Ways to have fun with your leaf bashing

- Make mini natural bunting to decorate a den or tiny house.
- Learn more about the plants in your area by making a plant identification guide washing line.
- Make pennants for a jousting tournament or marker flags for a little boat race (see page 60).
- Design a retro bike flag – attach a pennant to a long piece of basket willow and fix it to the seat post of your bike with masking tape.

Necklaces and pendants

For a long-lasting memory of a special day out, why not make a piece of jewellery from the natural materials you find?

Wooden beads

These can be made really simply from wood that has very soft pith, such as the elder tree. The pith can be poked out with a tent peg or small stick to create a hole to thread your necklace string through. You can also drill a hole lengthways into a stick and then saw off small sections to thread onto a cord.

Felt balls

If you are anywhere near sheep or goats in the summer you may be able to collect small amounts of the wool that they shed to make into felt. To make a felt bead, you just need to comb your wool or tease it apart as much as you can then make it into a large, loose fluffy ball. Wet your hands and rub a little soap on them, then start rolling the ball gently in your palms. As the wool gets wetter and warmer, it will clump together and the ball will get smaller. As it does, you can start to press harder to eventually make a small, hard ball of felt. To add it to a necklace, you can thread the bead onto a cord using a needle.

Witchy stones or hag stones

These are flint nodules with small holes in them. They can sometimes be found on flint beaches and are considered lucky in some places. If you hang them on a string outside your house or around your neck they are said to protect from sea witches in a storm! Whether you believe that or not, small ones are a rare find and make a really special necklace.

Artist's charcoal pencil

Charcoal is great stuff to sketch with. You can pick out cold, partially burned wood from an old fireplace or make your own in a tin on the fire.

You will need
- Metal tin with tightly fitting metal lid
- Hammer
- Nail
- Pencil-thick softwood twigs, e.g. willow
- Secateurs/knife (see page 16)
- Fireproof gloves/long sticks
- Wet clay
- Elder branch (optional)
- Tent peg (optional)

STEP 1
Poke a hole in the lid using a hammer and nail.

STEP 2
Using your secateurs or knife (see pages 20–23), cut some pencil-thick twigs of a fairly soft wood. Willow is common on riverbanks and in wetlands around the world and if you can find some, it makes the best charcoal for drawing. If you cut it in the spring or summer, it is very easy to peel the bark off, but don't worry if the bark is stuck on, it doesn't make a huge difference to its ability to draw.

STEP 3
Cut the twigs to the length you want with secateurs or your knife.

STEP 4
Lay or stack them in the tin. Fill it up but make sure that the lid can still fit on tightly.

STEP 5
Place the tin on the fire using fireproof gloves or long sticks.

STEP 6

Watch the thick white smoke and steam billow from the hole in the lid. When it changes to a wispy blue / grey colour, carefully remove it from the fire using fireproof gloves. This process depends on lots of things, such as the heat of the fire, and type, size and freshness of the wood, but should take about half an hour.

STEP 7

Bung the hole in the lid with some wet clay – don't touch the metal with your fingers.

STEP 8

When the tin is cold, open the lid and empty out your artist's charcoal.

You can draw with it as it is or make a pencil like this...

STEP 9

Cut a section of branch from an elder bush and use a tent peg to poke the soft pith back into the branch.

STEP 10

Select a straight piece of charcoal that will fit into the hole in the branch and carefully push it in.

STEP 11

Whittle (see pages 20–23) the end of the branch to sharpen it like a pencil.

Games and stories

Conkers

Conkers is the name of a classic game as well as the name of the seeds with which it is played. Shiny brown and waxy, the conker is the seed of the horse chestnut tree (*Aesculus hippocastanum*). It is native to a small area of the Balkans but you can find it in parks and city streets across the northern hemisphere.

Conkers was widely played in school playgrounds in Britain through the 19th and 20th centuries but seems to have faded in popularity. Claims that it had been banned on health and safety grounds turned out to be a myth and there is no need for specialist personal protective equipment when playing conkers.

Find a conker tree in September or October when the nuts are falling to the ground. Carefully open the prickly cases and take out the shiny, smooth brown seed. Fill your pockets but leave some for other conker hunters or you may not have any opponents to play against.

Drill (see pages 18 and 22) a neat round hole through the conker with a gimlet, palm drill or even a nail. Thread a strong string or shoelace through the hole and tie a knot at the end to secure the conker.

Tip

Hardening conkers is frowned upon by adults in competitions but trying to make the perfect indestructible conker is all part of the fun. Soaking in vinegar or baking in the oven are legendary ways to give your conker the consistency of granite.

How to play

The object of the game is to smash your opponent's conker to pieces and inherit its points. For example, if I beat six other fresh conkers, mine becomes a sixer. If I am then beaten by someone with a two-er, their conker becomes an eighter... and so on.

It is a good idea to always have a couple of turns of string around your hand to hold the conker steady on impact.

One player holds their conker hanging very still and the other takes a turn to strike it. Take turns to strike until one conker breaks and there is a winner.

Treasure hunts

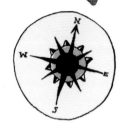

Use these simple ideas to start with or make up your own lists for your friends to find and do. Treasure hunts can be competitive or cooperative. If you are roaming far, it is best to stay in pairs and to set a time limit on the hunt or you might be out all night.

You can complete a whole list and come back when you have found everything. Or, you can read out one item at a time and only tell people the next thing when you have been shown the last item. If you start designing more elaborate treasure hunts, you might need to make a map or even hide some objects in advance.

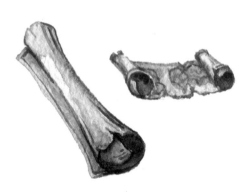

Finding things

Decide whether you are bringing the actual things or ticking them off a list when you have found them.

- Something springy
- Something wet
- Something sticky
- Something edible
- Something really heavy
- Something prickly
- Something delicate
- Something that smells beautiful
- Leaves from five different trees
- Something dead
- Something you think is treasure
- Something that is unique to you
- Something you know someone else will enjoy
- Something funny
- Something you would like to keep in your pocket for weeks

Doing things

- Follow an insect as far as you can
- Build the tallest tower of sticks
- Get your feet wet
- Spot a squirrel
- Dangle from a low branch
- Sit somewhere without moving for ten minutes
- Find a boomerang stick
- Make muddy hand prints
- Leave a place in a better state than you found it
- Leave a trail for other people to follow
- Interview a stone and report back what it said
- Dig a hole and bury one foot
- Talk like a bird
- Adopt a pet rock
- Take some litter home for recycling

If you have collected lots of natural things, try making them into something like a mandala (see page 76) or arranging your collection into a micro museum.

Spell ingredients and poems

Being creative with words is easier when you are surrounded by the great variety of different sounds, textures, smells, colours and patterns that you find when exploring outdoors. Your nature diary (see page 74) doesn't need to be an essay or a tick list – if you like, it could be a spell book.

Instead of collecting things, try collecting words as ingredients for poems or spells. What unusual interesting adjectives can you think of to describe what you see and collect? How can you use them in your writing to make your spell even more magical?

Choose an animal, a tree or a special place and watch for a while. Lots of the other activities are about getting to know your local nature. What do you notice when you try forest bathing (see page 154) or leaf bashing (see page 102)? Could you describe that experience in a poetic way?

If you abandon all the rules, you know then it will be impossible to get it wrong! If you would like to have a structure, you could start with a descriptive list of what is around you:

- Gnarly oak
- Distant buzzard
- Still water
- Mesmerizing flames
- Sunlit smoke

.... Build from there and see where the words take you.

Storytelling

Once upon a time, the tribes passed on their stories around their evening fires… But, the world became busier, people built houses to live in, grew crops in fields, drove cars on roads and eventually spent their time watching television and playing computer games. They didn't sit around fires telling stories as much as they used to but they never forgot the power of the campfire story.

Keep the old stories alive and bring new ones into life. Telling stories to others can be fun but it takes practice and confidence to speak in front of other people. If you have a tale that you want to learn so that you can tell it again and again, here are a few tips that might help:

- Write a list of words to remind you of the order of key events.
- Draw a picture with all the elements of the story in it.
- Use your own words to tell the story.
- Practise telling it to a toy or the fridge when there is no one else around.
- Smile or frown for emphasis when you talk.
- Give some characters silly voices or catchphrases.
- Move your hands and body to help express emotions and actions.
- If you forget something, don't worry, just make it up.

Telling stories with other people is a different matter, so why not try these ideas to make your own stories.

Round-robin story

Choose someone to start the story with a dramatic first line and then take it in turns to add the next sentence to build up a weird and wonderful chronicle. We have very few rules, apart from everyone should try to help the story grow, and that portals to other dimensions are definitely banned! It can be good fun to just add a single word each turn but the faster it gets, the more difficult it is and the weirder the results.

Send characters on a quest

Create a few characters from things that you find or make some forest friends (see page 68). Draw faces on them or add a few sticky eyes, give them names and roles in the story. Decide on a quest for the characters to embark on, throw in a few obstacles to get in their way and perhaps some magical animals or objects that could help them get past the things in their way. Cut a long length of string to lay out as the line for your story. Try to use the land around you to create a mini landscape for the quest. Move along the story line as you make up the tale and practise it a couple of times before you perform it to others.

Sound mapping

We often just notice the things that we can see and miss things by not fully using our other senses. The world can be a noisy place with lots going on but we need to stop and use our ears to pay attention for a while. It isn't easy to sit still in one place and just listen, but making a map of what you can hear will help you to focus and notice the sounds around you.

Find a spot that appeals to you and sit down in a position you find comfortable. It can be helpful to take a small mat to sit on and to lean your back against a tree. Settle down and try not to move your body too much.

Mark a cross in the centre of a blank piece of card – this represents the place where you are sitting.

Pay attention to what you can hear all around you. Use cupped hands to make your ears wider and amplify sounds in front of and behind you.

Draw something to represent the sounds that you hear. It doesn't have to be pictures of the things that make the sounds. Place them on the card in the direction that you hear them. There is no right or wrong way to do this and you will end up with a very personal record of the soundscape around you as you sit in your environment.

Skimming stones

You come across a stony beach next to calm, flat water. There is only one thing to do – skim some stones. Stone skimming is like learning to whistle or ride a bike: it takes lots of practice and failed attempts then, all of a sudden, the magic happens. Once you can skip a stone twice, keep practising and adding bounces until you can break the world record.

The World Stone Skimming Championships take place in September each year on Easdale Island in Scotland. The winner is the one who can consistently skim a stone to hit a cliff at the end of a narrow course. The world distance record event is held in Wales and stands at 399ft 6in (121.8m) for men and 172ft 3in (52.5m) for women.

The North American Stone Skipping Association plays by different rules and counts the total number of skips rather than distance. The world record for skips is 88.

Skimming tips

- It is much easier to skim successfully on calmer water.
- The best stones are fairly flat and measure 3–5in (7–12cm) in diameter.
- After a while, you will know a good stone when it just feels right in your hand.
- Stones with corners are good.
- The stone should roll along your index finger as you release it. Maximum spin will help the stone to keep skimming for longer.
- Releasing the stone at an angle of 20 degrees to the water is said to give the best results.

Pick a spot on the opposite bank or a stone in the middle of the water – see if you can manage to hit it repeatedly.

How far can you make the stone skip before it sinks? If you can, pace out the distance along the bank. Mark your farthest skim with a flag (see page 103) planted in the riverbank.

Count the number of skips your stone does before it sinks. Having a friend film it and play back slowly can help resolve any arguments!

Pooh sticks

Pooh sticks was invented in chapter six of *The House at Pooh Corner* by A.A. Milne in which Pooh discovers that fir cones float and rivers flow downstream. It is quite simply a stick race under a bridge.

How to play

All the players line up on the upstream side of a bridge and hold their sticks out over the edge. Don't lean so far out that you might fall in!

Check what everyone's stick looks like before the drop.

All players' sticks should be dropped (never thrown) from the same height, and at the same time, into the stream on the upstream side of the bridge.

Whose stick comes out first? They are the winner.

Pooh asked lots of interesting questions about floating things down rivers and it does no harm to try to find the answers for ourselves.

- Will a big stick travel faster than a small one?
- Do sticks always take longer than you would expect to travel under a bridge?
- Can you move a stick in the river by throwing stones on one side of it to make waves?

Why is this such a timeless and fascinating game? No one knows, but it is, so we are duty-bound to keep playing it whenever we come across a bridge.

Below left: The actual Pooh sticks bridge is a footbridge that crosses a tributary of the Medway in Posingford Wood, Sussex.
Below right: Why not try making and racing some little boats (see page 60)?

Tip

Stay aware of other bridge users when crossing the bridge and watch out for floating donkeys!

Ancient tree hunt

Go out and meet some amazing trees – trees that make you say 'Wow'! There is no exact age that a tree needs to be to qualify as ancient. Those that have lived an exceptionally long time for their species will probably have ridged, gnarly bark, be short, wide and might have a hollow trunk. They are home to a huge range of other plants, fungi and animals and are really important habitats.

Are there any stories associated with your particular tree? Can you find out a story from the year that your tree was planted?

You can search for the most amazing tree in your area or look up those already found on the world monumental trees inventory or the UK ancient tree inventory (see Resources, page 156, for links).

Not all amazing trees are ancient. Champion trees are the tallest or widest of their species in a particular area.

How old is my tree?

If you are not able to count the rings on the stump of a felled tree then you will need to do some sums to estimate how old the tree might be. There are so many different factors involved in the growth of any plant that it will only ever be possible to roughly estimate the age.

The first step is to give it a hug. How many hugs does it take to get all the way around the tree? Your hug is the same distance as your height, so to find out the circumference, just multiply the number of hugs by your height in feet or metres.

We need to know the radius of the trunk (half its width) so divide the circumference by 6.28 (2 pi) to find that measurement.

Find an old tree stump to see how wide an average growth ring is to work out how many would fit into your radius measurement for an estimate of the age of the tree.

Sit for a while at the foot of an ancient tree and imagine what might have happened here since it was a tiny sapling.

A gruesome tree tale

Judge William Hankford was a senior judge in 14th-century England under the rule of King Richard II, King Henry IV and Henry V. He was a melancholy man and apparently wanted to end his life but couldn't do it himself. He had a problem with poachers on his estate and he ordered his gamekeeper to sit in a big oak tree at night with his bow and to shoot any intruders without fear of blame. Judge Hankford then dressed in a dark cloak, walked out towards the tree. When he refused to identify himself, the keeper, who didn't recognize his master, shot and killed him. The story lives on with this amazing ancient hollow oak tree on his old Devon estate.

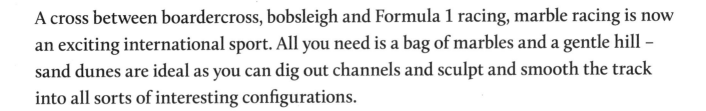

Marble racing

A cross between boardercross, bobsleigh and Formula 1 racing, marble racing is now an exciting international sport. All you need is a bag of marbles and a gentle hill – sand dunes are ideal as you can dig out channels and sculpt and smooth the track into all sorts of interesting configurations.

Don't worry if you don't have a handy sand dune, you can use a pile of earth to make a short track or collect sticks, rocks, bits of wood and even guttering to make a track on any surface.

Start simply with a few turns and high-speed straights then try building in splits, narrow sections, sharp turns, jumps and, of course, stands for the thousands of spectators.

Make a start gate and finish line. How will you make sure that all the marbles are released at the same time? Can you decide on the winner in a photo finish?

Choose marbles that are easy to tell apart and give them team names. If you want to do a running commentary, it makes the races even better.

May the best marble win!

Tip

If you are track building on sand or mud, then a small spade or trowel is useful to smooth the track. But you can dig and smooth using your hands, too.

Twig in your wig

This is a guessing game that will test your plant identification skills. Everyone playing should be wearing a nature crown (see page 50).

How to play

Each player secretly picks a leaf and places it in the crown of the person to their left. The aim is to guess what type of leaf has been put in your crown by asking 'yes' or 'no' questions to the rest of the players. Asking about colour, shape and size are good things to start with.

Exploring

Identifying plants

Knowing a bit about the different plants that grow in your area is really important to your adventures. Plants are interesting in themselves but if you want to make natural craft, you will need to find out what is going to be a useful material and recognize it, as well as knowing where and when it is okay to harvest it.

People learn in different ways but it is always easier if you need to know something for a good reason. Here are some tips on how you might learn about plants.

- Focus on one plant at a time. Make it something that you see regularly and is common to where you live. If it is something that you can use for a craft project, even better.
- Find out its different names. Maybe use one as your computer password for a few days (don't tell anyone!) until you have memorized it. I also change my desktop background picture to an image of the flower or leaf for the same time.

- On trees, the bark, leaves, buds and twigs may be really important clues to identifying them at different times of year. What do those different parts feel and smell like? Listen to the sound of the leaves rustling – not all trees sound the same in the wind. What shape are the leaves? Stand far away and see if you can spot your tree when it is growing with others.

- Get up close to the plants. Use all of your senses.
- Lots of plants have legends about them. Discovering their stories turns them from strangers into old friends. It won't be long before you have quite a few new friends in your local plant community and can start to tell others about them.

Stargazing

In the last 100 years it has become harder and harder to get a good view of the night sky because of all our electric lights shining up into space. To share a view of the galaxy that our ancestors took for granted, you will need to turn off the lights and look towards the darkest parts of the sky. If you can get far away from towns and cities, even better.

How you will see the stars depends on where in the world you are. It is amazing that one of the things that makes our home place unique is the light shining towards it from millions of light years away.

You don't need a telescope to enjoy stargazing, just take a blanket or tarpaulin to lie down on, look up on a cloudless night and marvel. Use a pair of binoculars for an awesome close-up view of the Moon or to see details like the different colours of stars.

People say that you should make a wish on every shooting star so, for a hatful of wishes, get out and look for the Perseids and Leonids meteor showers in mid-August and mid-November.

Names of stars

You might already know some of the common names given to constellations, based on Greek and Roman mythology, but see if you can find out their names and stories from other cultures that have their own history of astronomy. For instance, Inuit call the North Star *Nuuttuittuq*, the star that never moves. Tongans call it *Tuinga ik*a and in Arabic it is النطاق (*al-Nitāq*).

Of course, you don't need to know any of these names, it can be the most fun to just make up your own names for the patterns of stars you see in the sky.

Pond dipping

If you have tried invertebrate hunting under rocks and stones, you will spot some similarities with many of the creatures that you will find living in freshwater lakes, ponds and rivers. You may also find amphibious creatures and fish if you are lucky. It is really important to try to look after all the living things that you find and make sure that they are only disturbed for a short time while you look at them.

You will need

- Some sort of a net with a handle – you can get them in seaside shops or from tropical fish suppliers.
- A deep tray to empty the net into – an old baking tray or plant seed tray is ideal.
- A small spoon to pick up individual organisms and transfer them to a paint tray, yogurt pot or small bowl.
- A magnifying glass – I don't use much technology outdoors, but one fantastic thing to use is the phonescope, which is a microscope that clips onto a mobile phone and means that you can take close-up photos and videos of microscopic pondlife.

Choose a place where you can safely work without risk of falling into the water. Scoop up some pond water in your tray before you dip. Sweep the net around in the water, stirring up some of the sediment at the bottom if you can.

Empty the net into your tray of water. It will probably be fairly murky so let it settle while you rinse out the net in the pond to make sure that nothing is trapped in there.

Carefully move any leaves or plants in the tray and pick out individual invertebrates to have a closer look at and identify if you wish. As soon as you have finished, lower the animal back into to the water. Try not to drop or pour them in.

Staying safe at the water's edge

- Don't go pond dipping on your own and make sure that an adult knows where you are and what you are doing.
- If you have any cuts on your hands, cover them with plasters or thin gloves.
- Sitting or laying down when you are dipping is much safer than standing up.
- Avoid leaning over steep banks. Try dipping from the shallows or even a purpose-made pond-dipping platform.
- Keep a long rescue stick or rope nearby so that you can help anyone who ends up in the water without having to get in yourself.

Tip

In the summer, look out for the larval cases of dragonflies and mayflies on stems of water plants where they have emerged from the water.

Finding north with trees

Practising reading the signs in nature isn't so much about helping you if you get lost as it is about feeling at home where you are. Reading the world around you like a map gives you confidence in just being where you are and in getting wherever you want to be.

There are a few patterns and signs on trees that can help you to orientate yourself. Spend some time checking if that's true in your area and see what other patterns you notice where you live.

Moss on trees

It is often said that moss only grows on the north side of trees in the northern hemisphere and the south side in the southern. It is true that moss will thrive in cool, shady places but if you look carefully you will see it on all sides of trees as long as they can hold enough water there to survive. There is likely to be a dominant side, however, so you can at least use that information along with other clues to find north.

Exposed trees, especially in windy places, will likely bend away from the direction that the wind usually blows from. What direction is this where you live?

Sunny leaves and shady leaves

The same tree will often have different-sized leaves growing on its shadier and sunnier sides. Larger leaves on the shady side or nearer the trunk have a bigger area to catch sunlight and photosynthesize, creating food for the plant. Smaller leaves are on the sunny side of the tree.

Reading tree rings

If you come across a tree stump on your adventures, stop for a while and see if you can learn anything from it. Everything that happens to a tree leaves a mark on its rings – learning to read them can open the doors to the history of that tree's life.

In the middle of the circle of rings is the pith. This is the oldest part of the tree. Around it are rings of wood. Each ring is divided into a wider pale part, which grew in the spring and summer, as well as a narrow, darker coloured part, which grew in the autumn. Together they are one year's growth. Count these rings out from the pith to find out how old your tree was when it fell. Now work out the year it was planted. Can you find the year you were born?

You might notice that not all of the rings are the same size. The width of a ring can tell us about the weather in that year. Trees will grow more when it is warm and there is enough water in the soil. In a very cold or very dry year, the rings will be thinner. Read the rings to guess what the weather might have been like in the year you were born. Now ask yourself these questions:

- Is the pith exactly in the middle of the trunk? If so, the tree probably grew tall and straight.
- Are the growth rings wider on one side of the tree than the other? Narrow rings face into the wind or uphill on a leaning tree.

- Can you see any other clues in your tree stump? Are there any signs of branches, or damage from fire or animals?

If your tree stump has just been cut then, just for fun, get your nose close in and give it a good sniff. What does it smell like?

Cloud spotting

We usually walk along looking ahead or at the ground but sometimes it's good to just gaze upwards and have your head in the clouds. Depending on where you live you might see clouds every day or maybe just at certain times of the year.

Psychologists have discovered that if you are having trouble concentrating on a task, you can get back on track by spending a short time outdoors and looking at something natural that is fascinating and has lots of variety, such as trees, clouds or a babbling stream.*

Lie on the grass or a blanket, or just gaze out of the window and give your full attention to what you see in the sky. This can be calming if you are on your own but finding shapes in fluffy cumulus clouds and pointing them out to friends is great fun too.

Clouds are named by their shape and the height in the sky that they occur at. Not just ever-shifting and interesting to look at, they also provide lots of information about what is happening in the atmosphere and can be used to help predict what the weather might be in the next few hours. A few examples from each level of the atmosphere are shown below.

Cumulonimbus clouds are the towering, anvil-shaped storm clouds that can bring hail, thunder and lightning. They can store huge amounts of energy and be as much as 12½ miles (20km) high.

Norse myths...

...tell of the god Thor riding from his home in Asgard on a chariot pulled by two goats, the rumbling noise and sparks from the wheels being heard and seen by humans below as thunder and lightning. If you hear Thor's chariot, it is time to take shelter inside a building or vehicle.

Low-level clouds include cumulus and stratocumulus. These are the stereotypical little fluffy clouds.

Some typical medium-level clouds are altocumulus. 'Lenticular' or lens-shaped clouds are a variation that can form near hills or mountains.

High in the sky you can find cirrus uncinus – this name in Latin literally means 'curly hooks' but they are usually called 'mare's tails'.

*Kaplan, R., Kaplan, S. *The Experience of Nature: A Psychological Perspective*, Cambridge University Press, 1989.

*Seek out racing clouds on
a windy day. Are the high and low
clouds moving at the same speed?*

*Can you imagine other worlds high
above in the cloudy skyscape?*

*Are the types of clouds different if the wind is blowing
in a different direction from usual?*

*If you keep watch for a few hours, you might
notice cirrus giving way to altus and then cumulus
clouds. This is a sign of a warm front
approaching – you might want
to get your raincoat on.*

Track casting

As you explore an area, you will start to get to know the paths and trails made by other people, pets and wild animals. Going out first thing in the morning can be exciting and may reveal the news of what happened there the night before.

Look for signs like trails of flattened grass, lines of lower growing vegetation which has been trampled, slides down banks, gaps under fences, hair caught on barbed wire, latrine pits, scat (poo) and scratch marks.

If you want to capture the tracks or footprints of the animals in your area you will need to look for places on their usual routes where prints might be left behind. Dried-up puddles, muddy or sandy riverbanks and molehills are all good places to check.

If you can't find any prints then you can prepare the ground on a track in the evening and check it in the morning for prints. Use local materials such as soil from a molehill or just smooth some wet riverbank silt onto the path.

Unusual surfaces and human scent may disturb some animals and make them change their routes so take care, spend a bit of time experimenting and learn as much as you can about the behaviour of the animal whose track you are trying to capture. Avoid walking on trails yourself.

Once you have a decent imprint of a track, you can cast it in plaster to preserve it to study or as part of a collection.

Making a plaster cast

You will need
- Cardboard tube
- Plaster of Paris/dental plaster
- Trowel
- A small brush

STEP 1
Use a tube made from a piece of card, a cut-off coffee cup or a short section of drainpipe that will completely encircle the track and push it into the surrounding earth. It might be necessary to build up earth around the outside of the tube to seal it.

STEP 2
Mix some plaster of Paris or dental plaster according to the instructions on the packet and pour into your tube mould, making sure that all parts of the track are filled with plaster. The mixture will need to come at least ⅜in (1cm) above the top of the track to make a solid enough base. Let the mix set for at least half an hour before attempting to remove the cast.

STEP 3
Dig out the soil underneath the cast, rather than trying to just lift the cast from the earth.

STEP 4
Carefully pick away any soil and after a day or so, when completely dry, clean with a small brush under running water.

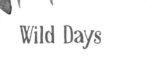

Listening to birdsong

You don't need to be an expert bird watcher to enjoy getting to know the birds in your neighbourhood. Everyone has to start somewhere and where better than out in nature, just sitting and listening. Your ears are as important as your eyes and often you will hear the songs and calls of birds that you will rarely see.

Understanding birdsong is not just a simple matter of matching sounds to a species. Patterns and variations in calls and the context in which you hear them can tell you lots about the birds around you, but also things like the presence of predators in the area.

Below: A yellowhammer singing.

Like learning any language, it takes practice. Some people find it easy and others nearly impossible. So, if you find it difficult to remember which birds are making the calls that you hear, don't worry about it. There is a lot to be said for keeping a sense of wonder at what you see and hear and not losing a little bit of it by naming everything or feeling like you have to become an expert. Enjoy asking the following questions...

- Can I see the bird making that call?
- Why might it be making that call?
- Can I follow its movements without scaring it off?

Can you make up a rhyme to remember the sound and rhythm of the song? 'A little bit of bread and no cheeeeeese' is a famous way of remembering the call of the yellowhammer.

Telling the time with a sundial

Sundials work by casting a shadow onto markings that have been measured to tell the time. Making a sundial is a good challenge and it can take a whole day if you want it to. Don't expect it to be very accurate at all – the nearest quarter of an hour would be pretty good going.

Above: The Jantar Mantar sundial in Jaipur, India is the world's biggest at nearly 90ft (27m) tall and accurate to two seconds!

You will need
- Straight stick, 3ft (1m) long
- Small sticks/stones
- Clock to accurately tell the time

STEP 1
Find a flat, open, outdoor area that has full sun all day. Bang a straight stick, about 3ft (1m) long, into the ground so that it isn't leaning left or right. Watch where its shadow ends then mark this spot with another stick or a stone. Make a note of the time from a watch or phone.

STEP 2
Keep doing this every 15 minutes or so and you will start to see a pattern emerge. What happens to the length of the shadow? If you manage to stay with this all day, well done! Come back and check the shadows and times in a few days' time. Are they the same as they were on the day you made the sundial? If not, can you find out why?

Finding north from your sundial

With five stones in a row, you can find true north. If you check with a compass, it will likely be a few degrees out as magnetic north varies from true north but if you are lost, it will be good enough to get your bearings. (For more ways to find north, see page 140.) Lay a long straight stick across all of the markers. This marks the passage of the sun from east to west. Now lay another straight stick perpendicular across the east west stick. This will show true north and south.

Butterfly science

Butterflies and moths are beautiful creatures with interesting life cycles and some very specific requirements for their food and habitat. We can learn a lot about the health of the wider environment by recording where, when and how many of the many different species we see. So get out your nature diary (see page 74) or a butterfly book and start counting.

There are conservation organizations working to protect butterflies all across the world. Find out which ones work in your area and see if they need any help counting and recording your local lepidoptera*.

You might need to download an app or print a recording sheet, then you can find a good spot to sit and note which species you see. Some surveys can happen in a back garden or a park, others involve going to a particular place to collect regular information about how numbers of butterflies change there. Even if you just learn a little bit more about these amazing insects, you will be doing something to help them survive and thrive.

To attract more butterflies to your local area, plant some of the nectar-rich plants they need for energy and the food plants that they lay their eggs on.

* Lepidoptera is the order of insects that includes butterflies and moths. They make up 10 percent of all species of organisms on earth and there are at least 180,000 different species already known.

Bug hunting

Some people call them minibeasts. I prefer their proper name – invertebrates. Reach over your shoulder and feel the middle of your back – those bumps are the bones in your spine. They are called vertebrae and they make up your backbone. The creatures we are going to go looking for don't have one. That's why they are called invertebrates and they make up 97 percent of the animal species on earth.

If there are so many of them, then surely they should be pretty easy to find? Well it depends where you look. Most invertebrates live in water for all or part of their lives (you find them by pond dipping – see page 138), but there are still plenty flying in the air and crawling on the ground.

You don't need much equipment, but if you want to study the animals you find up close then you will need a bug pot with a magnifying glass lid. It is a good idea to have a spoon to pick up small animals so that our fingers don't damage them. A fold-out guide or identification book will help you to find out what you are looking at.

Try sketching the animals that you find in your nature diary (see page 74). Looking carefully and drawing what you see is a great way of learning more about invertebrates and their lives.

Where to look

Reach over logs and stones to lift them up away from your body. Peer underneath and see what is trying to scuttle away from the light. Gently put anything you have lifted back where it was originally.

Most things you find will be harmless but if you live somewhere with animals that might cause you harm then make sure you ask an expert for advice on where to look and where to avoid.

Night-time nature hunt

If you want to get to know your local wildlife then you might need to head outside when the sun has set to look and listen for the nocturnal animals that we usually miss.

It is tempting to reach for a torch when you are exploring after dark but if you can do without it, you will experience so much more. Head out for a slow, careful walk somewhere without much artificial light and see how much night-time nature you can spot. Why not make a list of your findings in your nature diary (see page 74)?

What you might see

City foxes are much easier to spot than country foxes, and if you are lucky you might see a badger or a hedgehog.

Bats are always fun to spot. They occur in all the continents except the Antarctic and are mostly nocturnal creatures. Of the 1000 species worldwide, the majority of them eat insects and the rest eat fruit, frogs and even fish. Only three types eat blood from sheep, cows and horses – they are not keen on humans!

Watching bats is tricky as they are so fast, and most of us find it difficult to hear their calls. If you can find a building or tree where bats are living, the best time to see them is at dusk when they emerge from their roosts.

Invertebrates are the easiest living things to spot at night, but save this activity until the end of your walk, as you will need to turn a torch on if you want to see them. Find a spot with long grass or dead leaves on the ground. Point your torch straight down and turn it on. Slowly crouch down until the pool of light is all you can see. Lie down on your tummy and imagine that you are the size of millipede and start gently moving leaves, stones and grass until you find some of the millions of tiny creatures that live down here.

Above: Listen out for the distinctive calls of owls, and maybe spot the flap of a wing as one silently swoops past on its way to hunt.

Night vision

The retina at the back of our eyes is covered with cells called rods and cones that react to light in different ways. Cones are good at picking out colour and detail, whereas rods detect contrast and motion. At night, the cones are pretty useless but a chemical called rhodopsin floods the rods at night and makes them much more sensitive. However, rhodopsin is destroyed by light and takes at least half an hour to regenerate. If you wait half an hour in the dark, your eyes will adapt and you will be able to find your way more easily, though your vision will be black and white. As the rods are mostly around the edge of your retina, you will also be able to detect movement out of the corner of your eye better. If you turn your torch on or look at a phone then you will lose your natural night vision and have to wait for another half an hour.

Forest bathing

We all know that spending time outside is good for us. We get fitter walking and playing but we also often feel in a better mood from just being under the open sky. Forest bathing is an idea from Japan with lots of scientific evidence to show how being in the woods can help us all feel more relaxed, calm, alert and happy. Forest bathing activities are usually slow and quiet to help us notice things that we might miss when running, chatting and playing.

There are many ways to forest bathe. Here are just a few for you to try.

- Sit, leaning against a tree, and listen to what you can hear without thinking about home, school or friends.
- Dig a small hole in the earth with a stick and bury your feet, then sit and see what you notice for a while. You could also lie down with one hand buried in the earth, relax, and see what it feels like.
- Lie in a hammock looking up at the treetops moving.
- Walk along a path in silence, moving as slowly and quietly as you can. Pay attention to the smells of the woods and how they change.
- Find a beautiful view, sit and enjoy it.

Some of these ideas might seem a little unusual but they really do work to clear your mind, forget some worries and be ready for your next adventure.

Above:

In Japanese, forest bathing is called *shinrin yoku*. Look carefully at its Japanese characters - can you see a forest, a wood, and a valley with flowing water for bathing?

Resources

Online resources

Ancient trees
www.ancienttreeforum.co.uk
www.monumentaltrees.com/en/
ati.woodlandtrust.org.uk

Butterflies in North America
naba.org

Butterflies UK
butterfly-conservation.org

James Brunt (artist)
www.jamesbruntartist.co.uk

Land Art for Kids
www.landartforkids.com

Online storytelling course with Chris Holland
www.natureconnection.co.uk

Plantlife
plantlife.org.uk/uk

Richard Shilling (artist)
www.richardshilling.co.uk

Stellarium
Free open-source planetarium for your computer or phone.
stellarium.org

Stone skipping USA
www.stoneskipping.com

Tree age calculator
www.tree-guide.com

World Conker Championships
www.worldconkerchampionships.com

World Stone Skimming Championships
www.stoneskimming.com

Print resources

Forest Craft: A Child's Guide to Whittling
by Richard Irvine
(ISBN 978-1-78494-500-8)

Forest School Adventure
by Naomi Walmsley & Dan Westall
(ISBN 978-1-78494-403-2)

Hunter Gather Cook
by Nick Weston
(ISBN 978-1-78494-417-9)

Shinrin-Yoku, The Japanese Way of *Forest Bathing for Health and Recreation*
by Professor Yoshifumi Miyazaki
(ISBN 978-1-91202-369-1)

The Met Office Pocket Cloud Book
by Richard Hamblyn
(ISBN 13-978-0-7153-3761-5)

Acknowledgements

Thanks to:

Suzie, Jake and Stan for their constructive comments, testing ideas, joining in the photography, and all their unwavering support and encouragement. Marta, Zosia, Kesi, Mariama, Scotty and Josie for all being so photogenic. All the fellow educators and participants that have shared ideas and helped me develop my educational and woodland skills over the years. Hector Christie at Tapeley Park, whose woodlands help keep me sane. Red and Dan at Magdalen Farm in Dorset, who invented the game 'Twig in your Wig'. My professional 'family' in the Forest School Association Endorsed Trainers Group and the European Institute for Outdoor Adventure Education and Experiential Learning. Dominique Page, Commissioning and Senior Project Editor at GMC Publications, for inviting me to write and once again expertly guiding the whole process.

Picture credits

All step-by-step and styled photographs by Richard Irvine, and all backgrounds and illustrations by Shutterstock.com, unless otherwise stated.

Alamy Stock Photo: p.139; Alex Bailey (illustrations): pp. 24 & 26; Dominique Page: p.56; Megan Snyders (illustrations): cover, plus pp. 3–4, 31–32, 36, 50, 56, 74, 78, 98, 111, 114, 118, 130, 133, 154 & 160; Rebecca Mothersole: pp. 1, 4 (bottom), 5, 30, 33, 50 (top right), 51, 130–131, 134 (right) & 135; Robin Shields (illustrations): pp. 25 & 27–28; Shutterstock.com (photographs): pp. 2, 4 (top & middle), 7, 9 (middle left & bottom left), 11, 13, 15, 28–29, 37–39 (top), 50, 64, 72, 80, 104, 110, 112–113, 115–117, 119, 121–124 (bottom left), 125, 128, 132, 134 (left), 136–137, 140–143, 146–147, 150–154 (top right & bottom), 155–157 & 159; Stan Irvine (illustration): p.120.

Index

First published 2021 by
Guild of Master Craftsman Publications Ltd
Castle Place, 166 High Street, Lewes,
East Sussex BN7 1XU

Text © Richard Irvine, 2021
Copyright in the Work © GMC Publications Ltd, 2021

ISBN 978 1 78494 583 1

A catalogue record for this book is available from the
British Library.

Publisher Jonathan Bailey
Production Manager Jim Bulley
Commissioning & Senior Project Editor Dominique Page
Designer Claire Stevens

Colour origination by GMC Reprographics
Printed and bound in China

To order a book, contact:

GMC Publications Ltd,
Castle Place,
166 High Street,
Lewes, East Sussex,
BN7 1XU, United Kingdom
Tel: +44 (0)1273 488005
www.gmcbooks.com